Managing Your Energy at Work:

The Key to Unlocking Hidden Potential in the Workplace

By

Carol A. Bergmann

ISBN: 1-4107-5335-2 (e-book)
ISBN: 1-4107-5334-4 (Paperback)

This book is printed on acid free paper.

1stBooks - rev. 07/04/03

Acknowledgments

The process of bringing this material into written form has been a major journey spanning a good part of the last ten years of my life. Throughout this time there have been many who have supported me and contributed to the birthing of this material.

I express deep appreciation to all my colleagues, associates, and friends who have stood beside me as I have traveled down this path. Many have taken these concepts into their respective worlds and returned with insights that have added to the stories and brought greater clarity to the examples. They include: Barbara Braverman; Jonette Crowley; Dennis Fuhrman; Jill Gleeson; Michael Grich; Anita Halcyon; Jonathon James; Nancy and Eric Kirby; Doug Krug; Anita Laurence; Judith Light; Anne McGhee-Stinson; Ed Oakley; Larry Prochazka; Enocha Ryan; Pam Somers; Terah Stearns; John Vercelli; Arend Versteege; and, Sally and AG Wynne.

I especially want to thank my colleagues at Enlightened Leadership International, Inc. who have supported me as I fully utilized these concepts in all aspects of leadership. To authors Doug Krug and Ed Oakley, I acknowledge you for leading the way in bringing the importance of personal awareness into the realm of business.

Special thanks goes to: Marie Benesh and Kathy Wylie-Propersi in helping me formulate many of the key ideas for this book; Charlotte "Chickie" Hanin for always reminding me to trust my inner process; Sanford Jacobs for teaching me to open my heart and be vulnerable; MuJing Lau for being a student of life with me for yet another lifetime; and, G. Brock Nichols for standing by my side and encouraging me to "step out onto the dance floor."

Most importantly, I want to thank those who directly helped make this book reality. They include: my editor, Barbara McNichol, who patiently worked with me throughout the many versions of this book; my publishing consultant, Christine Testolini, whose coaching and direction opened my eyes to new possibilities, keeping my perspective clear and aligned; and, my colleague, Suzan Patrick, whose support and attention to detail kept me organized, focused, and sane. Thanks to all of you for your magic and insights in bringing this material alive.

Finally, I extend heart-felt thanks to my family who always supported me on my life path and to each person (a list too long to include here), who has touched my life and contributed to both my professional and personal growth.

IN LOVING MEMORY OF MY GRANDMOTHER

WHO FIRST INTRODUCED ME TO

THE MYSTERIES OF THE HUMAN SPIRIT.

This publication is intended to offer general information on personal and organizational effectiveness. Neither Aligned For Action, LLC nor the author is engaged in rendering psychological or medical services. If psychological, medical or other expert advice is needed or appropriate the reader is strongly encouraged to obtain the service of a professional expert.

TABLE OF CONTENTS

Preface

Much of the material in *Managing Your Energy At Work* was well underway when I read Margaret Wheatley's book *Leadership and the New Science: Learning About Organization from an Orderly Universe* (1994). I too pondered many of the questions she asks in her book, such as: "Why do so many organizations feel dead?" and, most importantly, "Why does change itself, that event that we're all supposed to be 'managing,' keep drowning us, relentlessly reducing any sense of mastery we might possess?"

For years, I searched for answers from inside the walls of organizations. There, working as a manager, leader, and at times an internal change agent, I searched for better ways to manage all the never-ending change around me. At the same time, I tried to attain the goals and objectives most often set by those in ranks higher than my own.

Sometimes I successfully reached those goals; other times I failed miserably (according to my own standards). As I reflected on a series of events, patterns emerged—patterns that occurred at a very deep level. As my awareness grew, I came to recognize, and later acknowledge, certain principles at work that we certainly don't learn in business school.

Interestingly enough, the answers to these questions came from a side of me that did not reside in the business world. Instead, they hovered in my private experience of personal development—the world where I explored my spirit self and asked, "Who am I?" This part of me did not feel valued and therefore was alienated from the world of business. If I acknowledged this—or allowed it to emerge in my work life—I believed I would be viewed as weak, not in control, not decisive enough. All these traits spelled trouble for a successful business career. The splits between these two realities seemed enormous at the time. So I kept my personal explorations quiet.

At the same time my business career was progressing, I fully dedicated my spare time to my own personal and spiritual growth. This path took me into the study of Eastern philosophies, including meditation and yoga. Through my practice, I soon learned that calming my mind drastically reduced my stress at work and outside of it.

This path also took me on a journey in which I explored many programs and techniques. As a result, I cleared one emotional blockage after another. After passing through each clearing, the world looked a little brighter to me. I would return to the "work grind" feeling lighter than I had left it, and could cope with its pressure more easily. The combination of the cleared blockages and calm mind allowed me to be more sensitive to the energies of those around me.

Then one day my two worlds collided. I was at the magical age of 40 when the crisis occurred—a physical breakdown. It appeared to be caused by enormous stress from leading a major business project. At the time, I believed I would bypass the trauma because of my strong pursuit of personal growth. However, fate has a funny way of catching up. I had no choice. I had to make peace with this new colliding reality. This realization has resulted in a slow integration that continues to this day.

After dealing with this life-changing crisis, I realized my need for control had shifted significantly. I came to see how it held me back, especially since I had always believed having control was a requirement to manage effectively. Coming to this realization brought joy and pain at the same time, for it occurred while I was leading a significant growth opportunity for my employer.

I suddenly felt like a three-legged colt with nowhere to hide. None of my experiences prepared me for this. Nor could I find others in my organization (peers or superiors) who could coach me through this revelation. It took months for my fear, mixed with a feeling of total isolation, to be slowly replaced with a new level of trust and peace that, frankly, I never thought could be possible in a business setting.

In retrospect, I fooled myself to think I could keep these two worlds separate. Like every being on this planet, I am energy–the essence of which we call spirit. My spirit automatically comes with me in the halls of my work life. And when I acknowledge its presence, the same miracles that occur in my personal life fill the space around me in the organization where I live.

This book explains the discoveries that put me on the path to understanding energy at work. I know I am certainly not alone on this journey. A broad sampling of business friends and acquaintances strongly indicates that conversations abound in the corridors of almost every organization concerning the need to acknowledge and express one's spirit in the workplace. Individuals *are* opening to new ways of experiencing life every day — and it is time embrace this in our organizations

It is my hope and intent that sharing these lessons guide other seekers who, like myself, listen to that voice within that says, "There is a better way."

Carol Bergmann
Denver, Colorado
November 2002

Introduction
Stepping Out

It was February of 1996. I couldn't put it off any longer. For months, I had a deep nagging sense it was time to leave my corporate job. The day came for me to explain why to my boss, the regional vice president of operations for a large computer services firm.

My successful career included twenty-three years of software development and management positions ranging from project management to human resource development. At the time I sat down in front of my boss to resign, I was the director of professional development working with management teams and their staff in several offices.

My boss Mike could be described as a "straight shooter." You know the type—quick, to the point, wants the "bottom line" result. Born and raised in New Jersey, Mike had little patience for "petty stuff." To me, his view of the world was black or white with few options in between. As his human resource director, I coached him on interpersonal matters with the management teams that reported to him. We got along

1

quite well—I know he respected my ability to turn around tough situations and give him insight into the human aspects of managing our region. I, in turn, respected his ability to lead and manage our region well.

That day, I sat before him clumsily putting words to something hard to explain. You see, I wasn't disgruntled or upset with my work. I wasn't leaving to take another job for higher pay or more opportunity. I wasn't even certain I was going to start another business—something I had done successfully in my early thirties.

All I had were the beginnings of a book and a vague idea that the answers I wanted could be found in the very process of leaving. Here I was, in the prime of my career, struggling to tell Mike I was driven by a voice within—the voice that kept saying I must leave to follow my heart.

Mind Drew a Blank

As I recall, I stuttered through the conversation. My mind drew a blank despite all my rehearsals. I was gripped by the realization that I couldn't turn back once I gave notice—and it severely compounded my problem. So I concluded my explanation with a pathetic "I'm not really sure why I am doing this."

Mike listened intently. "It sounds to me," he began, "that whatever you want to do isn't baked yet. You don't need to *leave*. You need to take a sabbatical, and get this thing out of your system. How long do you think it would take to bake this thing?"

I was in shock. It had never occurred to me to take a sabbatical. The voice inside specifically said I needed to leave *completely*. Yet, now facing this difficult scene, I wasn't sure about anything. I blurted out, "Probably six to nine months."

Mike showed his delight. "Then it's a done deal! You can take the sabbatical. We'll pull a person in from the field to cover your place and hold your position for you."

This all happened in the blink of an eye. Suddenly I was out the door and on my way to my hotel room with a splitting headache. I kept asking myself how this happened. Could a sabbatical truly fill the longing growing inside of me?

Follow My Inner Journey

The truth was: I *did* know why I was leaving! Yet no words could easily describe what had been taking place inside for the past several years. Since the early '80s, I had followed what could be called a spiritual quest. I spent my spare time reading everything I could, concerning the mind-body-spirit connection. I explored Eastern philosophies and Native American traditions. I went on shamanic journeys. I followed my intuition. As a result, my inner world became rich—filling a void that my career didn't reach.

Over time, I had successfully integrated this new learning into my work environment. For example, I fully used my intuition, which I'd learned to cultivate years before. I began to recognize the personal energy field around each person. When I facilitated team sessions, I could see how individual energy fields co-mingled to create a collective energy field. Miracles became a regular part of my workday.

Yet despite this integration of the unseen world of energy into my day-to-day activities, I felt alone. I couldn't share or talk about this; admit it was part of me or my success. I had to be careful to express my coaching or mentoring in terms of traditional processes. After all, I was a member of a management team representing the mission of the organization. But all this conflicted at a very deep level with who I had become. I could no longer hide it. Knowing the rules and respecting the organization, I had to leave.

Tell the Truth

That night, in deep meditation, I asked for guidance. The answer came simply and directly, "Go back to Mike and tell him the truth."

"Everything?" I asked. "Everything" came the reply. A great calm came over me.

The next morning I went into Mike's office, closed the door, and began to speak — this time without hesitation in my voice. I said, "Mike, I truly appreciate your offer for a sabbatical. I left your office last night shocked at my inability to explain why I am leaving. Worst of all, I lied to you. I fully know why I need to leave."

I told him about my dual lives and my spiritual journey and that, outside of work, I practiced astrology and gave intuitive readings. I also told him how this journey opened me to a new awareness of how people interact, including my ability to perceive personal energy fields.

These experiences forever changed my life by helping me see people and my work in a new way. "I don't expect you to understand all of what I am saying. But hopefully you can hear my excitement and see my congruency as I speak about this. I can't take a sabbatical; I know I am not returning — at least not in the kind of position I have served to date."

Mike sat back in his chair in intense silence and his eyes got wider the more I spoke. After a long pause, he carefully phrased his words, saying, "You know, a couple years ago I couldn't have handled this conversation. But the woman who is in my life now is into all of this. I am beginning to believe there is something to it all."

In my last two months of employment, my conversations with Mike were the most open I had ever had with him. To my surprise, they included questions he had concerning his own intuitive ability.

Why Women Leave

At the time I left my corporate position, a good friend and colleague Kathleen Wylie-Propersi was working on her Ph.D. dissertation. The topic: *Women Choosing to Leave Corporations for Self-Employment.*

Kathy conducted in-depth interviews with 12 female corporate managers who chose to leave the corporate world. Each interviewee explained a growing conflict between "who they were becoming" and "what they had to be" in the workplace. Several women described their experiences as *not having permission to be the person who was emerging within.*

As Kathy shared this with me, I saw myself more clearly. I, too, had wanted permission to express what I had become. Yet I was puzzled. Permission was *never* something I looked for in the past; I always believed it was my responsibility to take it when necessary. Why would I suddenly need permission in this situation?

Though I had done much to open and embrace my inner wisdom, I stopped dead in my tracks, unable to speak my truth—even when I felt determined to leave the organization and had nothing to lose. What had held me in its grip?

Three Distinct Areas

After taking time in the following months to determine the true answer to this question, three distinct areas of consideration emerged.

The first area reflects a cluster of fears that began simply as, "I will be ridiculed." Then it moved to a much deeper fear that directly attacked my identity, as in, "all that I have worked for in twenty three years could be wiped out in an instant."

Secondly, I struggled with how to use language to say what I wanted to say. Little to no context exists to speak on the topic of heart or soul in business. Following one's "gut" feeling is okay only as long as it's substantiated with hard facts.

Following one's heart—well, that is a different matter all together. To complicate the matter, the language familiar to those on an inner quest sounds "soft."

Listening to one's inner voice, following one's heart, quieting one's mind, creating safe space for others, opening, centering, and being—these words seem soft in harsh contrast to business terms—the bottom line, accountability for results, thinking, controlling, and implementing. Like emotions that rarely have permissible expression in business, words of the heart and soul sound weak to those steeped in business acumen.

Language provides the window into the deeper level of beliefs and culture. Knowing this, the third area should not have surprised me. Yet, it bothered me the most. *I realized I still bought into the established culture.* This revealed the real need for me to leave the corporate environment. It also was the answer to the voice within that said, "Only in leaving completely would I understand." I believe this insight forms the core of the permission issue and requires answering a new question, "How can *I* make a difference in this whole culture?"

Now Waking Up

I am not alone in this. Many people are now "waking up" to their own inner awareness, as evidenced by a survey published in American Demographics (Ray, Paul H. "The Emerging Culture." *American Demographics*, February 1997). The author described what many have known for some time—a major shift in values is under way in the general population.

Recapping data from an American LIVES survey conducted in 1994, Ray points out that nearly one-fourth of American adults (24 percent or 44 million) make up an emerging group labeled Cultural Creatives. This is added to Traditionals (29 percent or 56 million) and Moderns (47 percent or 88 million.)

Interest in spiritual values is increasing, evidenced by the tremendous growth in mind-body-spirit products and services—a market specifically created to address the needs of emerging Creatives. High on the list of important values for Creatives are altruism, self-actualization, and spirituality. "Creatives are forging a new sense of the sacred that incorporates personal growth psychology, the spiritual realm, and service to others," says Ray.

"Despite their numbers," Ray points out, "Cultural Creatives tend to believe that few people share their values. This is partly because their views are rarely represented in the mainstream media, which is mostly owned and operated according to the Modern world-view. Yet little of what they read gives them any evidence of their huge numbers."

Certainly this also applies in the halls of Corporate America. As people continue to explore their own inner beings *outside* of the office, the need to give voice to these new ways of being will become a requirement *inside* the office. Faced with the fear of being alone and the challenge of integrating this new awareness into their daily work, I believe dissatisfaction will keep rising among corporate citizens. Some will leave. Others needing the security of their jobs will feel trapped, causing productivity to drop.

So the questions remain: "What will it take to break through the barriers and begin to create a new, more supportive, culture within corporate organizations? To meet these challenges, what must we do differently?"

The Shift

The answer lies in not what we have to *do* differently; it actually lies in what we must *become*. It is the journey to return to our own source, opening to the expression of who and what we truly are. It shows up by learning to set our egos aside and look to an intuitive source within for the answers. That certainly goes against what many us, including our leaders have been trained to do.

Today, as indicated by the American LIVES survey, multitudes of people are opening to the idea that, as living breathing human beings, they indeed are much more than the body they occupy. So at the level of personal belief, many individuals are acknowledging the dimension of a spiritual energy that is a fundamental part of who and what they are.

Overview of *Managing Your Energy At Work*

Much material has been written for those to discover the unseen realms of energy within themselves and others. Yet, the concepts of energy's effect on the individual, groups and teams, and the organization as a whole, lack a presence in the work arena. Little has been written on energy as it pertains to the business environment.

This book serves as a guide for anyone in today's workplace who recognizes that a shift is under way. It specifically calls to leaders and managers in organizations to realize the emerging new way of being. More specifically, it provides insights for those who choose to listen to gentle pressures within telling them they need to find another way.

This book takes a new look at some of the most critical elements relied on in business. They include Intention, Commitment, Integrity, Trust, Communication and Intuition — all part of creating bottom-line results.

Chapter 1 begins with Energy, the source of all things. Before understanding how intention, commitment, integrity, trust and communication work, we must understand this unseen force that drives us all. It lays the foundation by explaining what energy is and how an increased understanding of it can change the way we view others and ourselves.

Chapters 2 and 3 define how we manifest results. Though much of business is driven by the bottom line, do we really know how results are created? Much is written about the need for commitment, yet the crucial role of intent is rarely discussed. Therefore, Chapter 2 explores this critical element of

Intention, explaining how it works in conjunction with commitment to manifest results. Many problems we face in the area of commitment are actually problems of intent. When we understand this we can get at the heart of problems that often plague the implementation of programs, projects, and change efforts, big and small.

Chapter 3 sheds light on the role of Commitment. A word used so commonly in business, yet it's a crucial element that often seems elusive—especially when needed most. This chapter defines commitment in terms of energy and discusses how to remove the blocks that inhibit it. It also offers ways to help promote and channel commitment through an organization.

Chapter 4 explores the many aspects of Integrity, a critical characteristic often associated with leadership. Although we often look for this characteristic in others, this chapter describes the inner exploration required to find it within ourselves. By quieting the mind and finding our center, we find the path that leads to our own expression of integrity. As we begin to understand our own inner being, we can actually accomplish far more with far greater authenticity.

Chapter 5 focuses on Trust, another critical element often misunderstood in business. This chapter makes a distinction between two forms of trust: one based on confidence and/or positive experiences that have been repeated over time; and unconditional trust that is not based on past experience. This chapter explores the prerequisites for this higher form of trust to emerge.

Chapter 6 looks at the importance of acknowledging Intuition as a key leadership skill. It takes a look at how we can cultivate intuition and use it successfully in the workplace.

Chapter 7 discusses how understanding energy changes the way we approach Communication. Thoughts precede words; words precede actions, the interplay between these three, forms the basis for daily drama in our world. These elements drive all business interactions and determine the precious results from which job performances are measured. Looking at communication from the perspective of energy, we see ways to solve the communication deficit that plagues our organizations yet is so critical in helping move individuals through the massive maze of change.

With a fuller understanding of the crucial elements, **Chapter 8** puts it all together. This chapter on Integration explores ways to apply these concepts in our every day work environment. It addresses how to manage our own energy and identifies ways to remain in the flow, even during the most stressful of times. Using actual examples, this chapter explains the importance of managing our own energy first, and then reveals its powerful effect on our work environment—both with ourselves, as well as, in the reality we face in our workplace.

Chapter 9 describes the New Role of the Leader. If we can only manage our own energy, what is the true role of a manager? What is different from what we have known in the past? This chapter answers these questions and further explores ways to lead from this new understanding of energy. With this learning we find new ways in supporting colleagues, employees, and even superiors. Finally, the chapter concludes by summarizing the benefits of embracing these concepts. Even the smallest shift in one's mindset can cause tremendous headway in dealing with the challenges we face in our organizations everyday.

The Rest of the Story

Leaving my corporate position provided the insights I needed to complete this work. It took me deeper into my own exploration of self. In addition, it also provided me the time to explore what others where facing in their world too. I worked with individuals—coaching mainly managers and leaders— who found themselves frustrated and looking for ways to emerge from the chaos that they were often facing in their business environments.

I returned to the corporate world two years later. Working as an executive of a training organization I was able to fully utilize the concepts and processes that are described in this material. Despite the challenges of the position, I experienced new levels of ease and inner peace that I had not experiences before.

The concepts in this book are not to be considered "the only way." Instead they are offered as a guide for those who are looking for new possibilities to rise above the chaos and seek the permission to express their spirit more fully in their workplace. In sharing these insights it is my hope that others may benefit by tapping into the hidden resources that are available to all.

Chapter One
Energy: The Source

I awake before dawn, knowing that within a few short hours I will be flying eastward, high above the earth, to my day's destination. I quickly shower, letting the warmth of the water center me before I rush into my final preparation and leave for the airport. I eat a hurried breakfast and get on my way.

As I pull out of my driveway, I remember to stop and fill up my car's gas tank, just in case I get caught in a morning rush hour traffic jam. But this morning, I am in luck. I make it to the airport with plenty of time.

By the time my plane takes off, the sun is rising over the Cascades mountain range. As my plane turns and banks around the majestic peak of Mount Rainer, I watch it head directly into the sun's light and warmth that is the source of fuel for life on this planet.

From our lessons in even the most basic physics, we know that fuel is stored energy. It waits for the appropriate catalyst or chemical reaction to release its power and utility. From the perspective of our senses, we see a reality filled with solid things. Therefore, we commonly perceive energy in forms that are familiar: light, warmth, and motion—just as I experienced while traveling.

However, Einstein's famous equation, $E=mc^2$, has forever changed our understanding of matter. Scientists say that on the subatomic level, our entire world is composed of energy, including every cell of our body. In addition, the space around us, once thought to be empty, is also alive with fields composed of particles of energy. The idea that we, as human beings, are solid separate forms is no longer valid. I believe our understanding of ourselves will shift dramatically as science unlocks the mysteries that await—not only in our bodies but in the realm of the human energy field.

While scientists redefine our view of reality, we're witnessing a marked increase in the numbers of people exploring the connection between mind, body, and spirit. This is evidenced by the tremendous growth in the products and services focusing on alternative approaches to health and peace of mind. The very fact that this fast-growing sector of the economy is still labeled "alternative" points to a separation between what has been mainstream and what is emerging.

Yet it is through this exploration of alternative forms of healing mind and body—coupled with the push to achieve inner peace—that we begin to experience our own bio-energy field. Despite these discoveries and the personal exploration so many have undertaken, we have yet to understand what this means in our organizations.

In my explorations of the human energy field—both through my own healing process and in my daily interactions at work—my perceptions have been heightened. As I have learned to embrace my own inner journey, my experiences of individual communication, team interaction, and group dynamics have all come alive. I see how the energies that each individual emits play and interact with each other.

This is a far contrast from my earlier days as a young manager in a corporate environment. My approach to my position was one of needing to have all the answers and dealing with the actions of colleagues and employees in a mechanistic way. Like many others, I believed I could manage people in the same way I manage tasks.

As my awareness grew, I began to realize how impossible that approach was! *Each individual can only manage his or her own energy.* Yes, I could influence others, but I couldn't *ever* manage their energies.

This understanding of human energy at a deep, respectful level has changed the way I approach every position I take on. It has shifted the relationship between the effort I expend to accomplish something and the results I create—dramatically reducing the amount of effort I once believed was necessary to be successful. Learning to tap into this potential is key to surviving the challenges in the hectic work environments we have come to accept as the norm.

The Challenge

In the last few decades, the amount of change has dramatically increased—not only in organizations but also in the world. The level of change any one individual must deal with has *itself* changed on several levels.

First, the *quantity* of change, from every direction, has greatly increased. Global competition has spawned the need to find better, faster, cheaper ways of producing goods and services. Advances in technology have provided ways to make all this happen faster. From the skills we need to the systems we interface with, from the tools we use to the ways we communicate, everything keeps changing. The message is getting out to every employee and company leader: *The only constant is change itself.*

Second, the *frequency* of change has increased significantly over the last several years. And intervals between major changes have dwindled to the point where it is difficult to distinguish between the beginning of one cycle and the completion of another. In fact, the whole concept of completion rarely exists within the walls of a typical organization today.

Third, the *scope or intensity* of change is also far greater than most organizations have ever experienced. With growth and the increasing popularity of re-engineering, "whole company change" has become a familiar — and often dreaded — process.

This third level especially has created an increase in the number of *significant emotional events* experienced by any one individual. In days gone by, emotional events sparking significant feelings of loss were confined to divorces and deaths in one's family. Today, significant losses occur frequently due to changes in the work environment. Downsizing has displaced thousands of workers, while advances in technology have pushed aside thousands more. They find themselves at a loss to get the work they were once skilled to do.

This dramatic increase in the quantity, frequency, and intensity of change places enormous challenges on leaders and managers who struggle to overcome them. Sadly, the strategies they turn to were developed in the past when the rules were radically different.

Today's challenge, then, becomes, "How can leaders and managers deal with the seemingly unending 'stuff' that comes up when their employees (not to mention themselves) face uncertainty, confusion, turmoil, and loss at work?"

Energy in the Workplace

Understanding energy in the workplace can be compared to the time when man first learned to fly.

For ages before the Wright brothers' famous flight, man tried to fly like a bird, not really understanding the principles that allowed birds to defy gravity. Only after aviation pioneers discovered the secrets of the unseen world of aerodynamics could they build a machine that flies. Simply stated, an airplane flies because it *uses* the forces of nature to leave the earth; it does not *oppose* those forces.

This applies to our work environments as well. The forces of nature are available all the time. Like the laws of aerodynamics, these forces or principles lie waiting to be discovered.

Understanding the unseen realm of energy and its principles gives us new capabilities to deal with a workplace filled with change. Leaders and managers responsible for guiding change in the workplace are wise to acknowledge not only the source of energy within themselves, but the energy emanating from people around them. The time has come to employ these forces in our daily work lives—to lead and manage by *using* the unseen forces available rather than *opposing* them.

So how does this elusive realm of energy operate in organizations today? If it is always there, how do we work with it consciously and tap into its potential?

Types of Energy

Energy can be grouped into two main categories: personal and universal. However, an important phenomenon occurs when individuals in a group channel their personal energies into a common cause or activity. It's called collective energy. The concept of collective energy is extremely important to understand in organizations; it forms the foundation of many theories in the areas of group, team, and organizational dynamics.

Universal energy surrounds us all—an invisible field constantly available to tap in to. It provides vital nourishment to supplement our own reserves of personal energy. When our personal energies flow freely, we open a channel for universal energy to flow into and through us. It may seem hard to believe but a simple request is all it takes for the flow to begin. Yet, to fully tap into this universal source, we must first understand how our personal energy field works so we can embrace the natural flow within us.

This book focuses on *personal* and *collective* energy rather than universal energy, for these are what we most encounter with others in the workplace.

PERSONAL ENERGY

Energy Created from Fuel

Every living thing radiates an aura of personal energy labeled "subtle" because people have difficulty perceiving it through their five senses. However, modern science can detect this energy field by various means, including the use of Kirilian photography. This technique actually takes a picture of a portion of the subtle energy field as it radiates from a living entity.

As a living entity, each person has a reserve of personal energy created from fuel consumed in the form of air, food, and water. If we think about it, the energy in our bodies actively creates and maintains our feelings of vitality. When we're filled with energy, we feel alive, active, able to handle anything that life presents. We exercise, socialize, organize, and analyze activities that produce some form of interaction with the world around us.

Common sense tells us that by maintaining a healthy diet and caring for our bodies, we can enjoy a vital reserve of personal energy. This is certainly true. In addition, our mental attitude affects the vitality and quality of our personal energies.

Thoughts Are Energy, Too

Every thought that goes through our minds, consciously or unconsciously, is a form of personal energy. Personal energy filters through our beliefs. Like a resistor that regulates the flow of the electricity when the current passes through it, so does a belief alter the intensity of the energy thought form sent into the world.

18

For example, a person who has beliefs that support a world filled with possibilities has abundant personal energy. In contrast, a person who believes the world is a difficult place finds the energy supply low. He or she may feel tired much of the time, despite efforts to maintain a healthy body.

This understanding of how our thoughts regulate the flow of our personal energy is key in learning how to truly reduce stress in our lives. Most often, people want to know how to reduce stress, establish a work/life balance, and create greater ease in the day-to-day grind where "doing more with less" is the corporate mantra. Understanding the power of our own thoughts — and their control over our reserve of personal energy — is at the very core of knowing how to deal with stress and change positively.

Managing Personal Energy

In the field of management, we tend to believe we are managing others. This often leads to misconceptions concerning how we manage people (and tasks as well) in an organization. From the perspective of energy, this is a misconception, for people can only manage their own personal energies, not the energies of another.

Having said this, it is just as important to understand that one can certainly *affect* the energy of another. This happens all of the time. However, this is different than trying to *manage* the energy of another.

To explain further, our personal energy fields extend outward from our bodies where they interact with the world around us. Understanding that our thoughts regulate the flow of these energy fields, we begin to realize that those who interact with us can perceive the attitude or beliefs we hold.

If our personal energy flows openly, others experience our energy as positive and supportive. They feel at ease approaching us. More importantly, colleagues and employees experience a sense of safety in speaking with us when we're in this state. This creates an environment that invites others to be open as well.

Conversely, if our personal energy is restricted, perhaps due to a judgments or limiting beliefs we hold, others experience us as draining or difficult to deal with. We may seem unapproachable or hard to get along with. A leader who functions in this state most likely creates an environment of fear and defensiveness in which others do not feel they have permission to speak openly.

As noted earlier, we *can* manage our own thoughts. Changing our thoughts, including the attitudes and beliefs we hold, alters our personal energy fields. Applied to the workplace, that means we have the ability to manage our *responses* to situations and the energy sent out by those around us.

Positive and Negative Forms of Energy

Like everything we perceive in this world of illusion, we likely experience things through polarities or opposites: black vs. white; right vs. wrong; up vs. down; night vs. day, and so on. So, too, is our experience with energy a bipolar one: positive vs. negative.

Each of us can easily recognize the radiant feeling we get when encountering someone filled with joy, someone openly displaying a love of living like a small child bubbling with the wonderment or innocence of living in the moment— spontaneous and free.

On the contrary, we may also recognize another person's energy as negative: someone who grumbles about life in general, who hates what he or she does, who blames others for all trials encountered.

However, the true opposite of positive energy (simply meaning energy which flows) is lack of energy. Those who complain and blame, for example, (often unconsciously) indicate that their energies are being blocked. When energy cannot flow, we experience its absence as being negative, just as we experience lack of light as dark.

Now, you may think of times when you are *certain* you witnessed negative energy at work. Thinking of such an occasion might make it hard to accept the idea that negative energy is nothing more than a lack of energy! As an example, consider an electrical short. At the point of the short, the flow of electricity is partially interrupted until the wire or connection breaks all together. When the break is only partial or the connection is intermittent, sparks fly in a burst of misdirected current or energy.

So it is with an individual experiencing a blockage of the normal flow of personal energy. A burst of misdirected energy occurs. This can show up as anger, defensiveness, jealousy, or insecurity, just to name a few possible emotions. We perceive and often label these reactions as negative. However, as our awareness of energetic forces increases, we recognize this actual blockage or lack of energy flow as fear.

Just as we experience fear when confronted with a grave situation like a shortage of air, the lack of energy flow on the subtle level also brings up fear. On a subconscious level, our minds, bodies, and spirits know that—just like the air we breathe—we require this flow of subtle energy for survival. Over time, a continued blockage of energy results in dis-ease and the eventual deterioration of the physical body.

As human beings we all participate in being blocked in some form or another. Interestingly enough, we have spent little time learning how to manage or work with our own energy field. Most often it is in situations where we interact with others that we have the opportunity to experience the emotional triggers of both others and ourselves.

Yes, the typical work environment provides ample opportunity to experience blocked energy. For instance, in one meeting I facilitated, I could "feel" the energy blockages before I even opened the session. It only took a couple of questions to ask what was really going on for the group. We identified that a few key players in the room believed the meeting would be a waste of time and didn't want to participate. This is only one small example of blocked energy. Throughout this book, we'll explore many more.

How Energy Blocks Set Up

A blockage in energy is created when people hold a limiting thought about themselves or others. If this thought is repeated over time, it forms a limiting pattern, called a (limiting) belief.

At the source of any belief (whether limiting or beneficial) is a decision made at some point in the past. Every decision we make becomes a fact in our personal view of the world, forming the basis of what we perceive as reality. Therefore, throughout our lives, we continue to see the world through the filters of past decisions and beliefs formed because of them.

Despite the myriad of beliefs we hold as true, rarely do we remember the actual source that caused us to create these beliefs. And yet they form the basis for how each of us develops our personal reality. Most often, these filters lie outside of our conscious awareness, so the core challenge becomes identifying (and then clearing) our blockages. We are usually blind to our own blockages yet painfully aware of the blockages of others!

Because we are rarely aware of how our own beliefs are operating, I like to refer to the limiting ones as *unconscious thought patterns*. I find that this reference helps me remember that something outside of my conscious awareness (or the conscious awareness of others) is at the cause of *any* negative reaction that might arise.

When we become aware of our limiting beliefs or unconscious thought patterns—and most importantly the decisions that created these—we gain a freedom to make new choices that can have a profound impact on our personal worlds.

A common belief that I often encounter is, "It takes a long time to change behavior." Behavior is often the by-product of the beliefs we hold. We try to change behavior directly when in fact the behavior is connected to a belief that drives it. The key is to identify the belief and the decision that formed it. Then, a new decision can be made.

Working with Your Blocked Energy

So the next question is, "How do I deal with a person whose energy is blocked?" Staying centered and in the present moment is the best insurance against the effects of blocked energy of others. This is far easier said than done; it assumes you have completed your homework and have spent time identifying and clearing your own unconscious thought patterns.

Critical for helping others work through their energy blocks is clearing your own blockages. Although this sounds like simple and sound advice, it is difficult to follow. Paradoxically, it is easier to see a blockage in another person then to look squarely into the mirror and face your own.

The first step in clearing a block within you is being aware of its presence. Many emotions help identify restricted energy flow, including feeling upset or resistant in reaction to some external experience, either a person or situation. Any emotional response that feels stressful is a major clue that something is not flowing in *your* energy field. Anger, resentment, jealously, resistance, pain, and hurt are some of the feelings that require attention.

If you remember an incident that brought up one of these reactions for you, you'll notice that your energy feels drained. You may feel stuck or tired. When you do something you really want to change but can't find the discipline for it, an unconscious thought pattern is likely at the source of the problem. A pattern develops and the behavior gets repeated; no matter how hard you *try*, you can't seem to break the habit or change the behavior. So identifying the limiting thought patterns that drive the behavior can provide the means to shift that behavior.

Again, the workplace is filled with opportunities to identify blocks within; a constant stream of "stuff" comes from every direction. Dealing with external demands and pressures often triggers reactions, appearing as if something external (a person or a situation) caused the reaction. Yet, the truth is that our "hot buttons" are only triggered if our own energy is blocked.

Choosing to Look Within

Each of us has a choice on how we view each experience we encounter in our work environment. We can either decide we have no ability to change the way we feel when faced with a difficult person or situation (believing that it is the other person or the situation that must change), or we can begin to look within ourselves for the source of the emotion or pain that we experience.

Early in my corporate career, I worked with an individual who had the uncanny ability to push my "hot buttons." We were required to work together on many projects. In my mind, she needed to control everything, which made collaboration a challenge, to say the least.

Whenever we had to meet on a mutual project, I dreaded it. I tried every strategy in the book to "deal" with her antics. First, I tried to be nice to her. That resulted in losing control of my side of the project. Next, I tried to "out control" her. That only caused her to manipulate situations behind my back. Then, I pointed out these difficulties to our boss. Despite her methods, she always managed to get the results our leader wanted, so my words fell on deaf ears. On and on, I wanted to outmaneuver her, all the time wondering how she managed to be a source of endless frustration to myself, and others.

Finally, I asked this question, "What was she mirroring that was blocked in me?" That led me to realize that I, too, had significant control issues. What I judged in her were some of the same things I had difficulty looking at within me.

Once I realized this, I began to approach her with respect and compassion, seeing an exaggerated version of my own behaviors. As I acknowledged her as a true gift to me, she could no longer press my "hot buttons." Because the "edge" was off, her response to me began to shift—cautiously at first, but it opened up little by little.

One day, I asked her to go to lunch (something I would never have done before my revelation). We had an incredible conversation that allowed us to find common ground working together. I must confess that she never became my favorite person to work with. However, I stopped expending all my energy trying to figure out counter strategies to work with her (definitely a personal energy drain). Instead, she became another co-worker in my office environment.

Identifying Unconscious Thought Patterns

Once you have identified an emotional reaction or trigger, you now have a pointer to lead you to the unconscious thought or block that restricts your energy flow. To get to the actual source of the block, use the following questioning process to open your unconscious.

Begin by recalling the situation that created the reaction. Once you recall it, ask, "What is the source of this reaction within me?" Be patient and trust the first answer that comes to you.

Most often, the source is a limiting decision or judgment made about the person or situation. Ironically, this decision often points to something the other person mirrors that you do not like about yourself. This was definitely true with my annoying colleague; I had made several judgments about her and her behavior, and especially her extreme desire to control—a behavior of mine I did not want to own.

Once you have an answer, take a moment to honor yourself for listening. This may sound like a simple or unnecessary step. Yet, honoring yourself for listening to your inner wisdom aids in opening the energy flow. And it counteracts a conditioning to push away or "stuff" unwanted reactions and behaviors when, in fact, they have served a purpose in the past.

Continue by asking, "What else is the true source of this reaction?" You may want to ask this several times. The first answer may begin to help you identify the source. Most likely, you can dig deep for more information. So again, be patient and continue the process until you feel you have tapped into the true source of the reaction, remembering to always honor yourself as the answer is revealed.

When exploring this line of questioning, you may get a sense of the core issue without fully getting to the underlying decision. When this occurs, ask, "What decision have I made about this person or this situation that caused the reaction within me?"

When you finally identify the decision, you may become aware you made this decision a long time ago about someone or something else; this person or situation has reminded you of that past event. This is the reason for calling it a limiting thought pattern, for we continue to repeat these reactions until we successfully remember the original source that set up the pattern (or belief) to begin with.

Many of our limiting decisions were made at a time when we truly did not have the understanding or wisdom we have currently. Knowing this makes it easier to identify the decision, honoring that we made it for a very important reason that made total sense at the time we were faced with the original situation.

PROCESS TO IDENTIFY AND CLEAR UNCONSCIOUS THOUGHT PATTERNS

1. Recall the situation that created the emotional reaction. Return to the feelings you experienced at that time.

2. Ask, "What is the source of this reaction within me?

3. Trust the first answer and thank yourself for listening.

4. Continue to probe deeper. Ask, "What else is the true source of this reaction?

5. Repeat Step 4 until you identify the true source of your reaction. Hint: The answer will be something deep within you (not caused by something external) and may be something you would never have thought of originally.

6. If the answer doesn't come in the form of a decision, ask, "What decision have I made about this person or situation?"

7. Once you have identified the source, you can make a new decision or choose a new behavior.

Once you have identified the actual source of this reaction, you now can choose a new decision or course of action. The key to clearing the block is getting to the *origin* of the reaction within you, not just the *symptoms* of the situation or the other person's behavior.

Although I have used this process many times on myself, I sometimes find it helpful to have someone "spot" me through it. When someone else asks the questions, I can totally focus on what is going on within me. Also, the human mind can be so conditioned to rationalize—looking for external reasons "why" something occurred—that it makes it difficult to find the true source of the issue.

COLLECTIVE ENERGY

Effects of Group Consciousness

As we begin to understand how our personal energy can be affected when others push our "hot buttons," we see collective energy at work. The interaction between two people is the smallest example of collective energy and can bring up areas unconscious to either party.

As we understand the power of accepting our own beliefs and thoughts as energy, we become aware of the power of acknowledging group or collective energy. It is here—on the collective energy level—that we begin to see the effects of group consciousness.

That which we call "culture" in an organization is made up of the shared beliefs and values of the leadership of an organization. In addition, this interaction of thought patterns and energy at the collective level impacts the overall quality of the collective experience in an organization.

For example, when doubt or mistrust begins to spread in an organization, we see low morale emerging as just one symptom of this collective thought pattern. By contrast, when collective energy is aligned and flowing in the organization, overall effectiveness and productivity increases.

So, to effectively manage or lead an organization, it is helpful to understand when to work with personal energy versus collective energy. In fact, like Christmas lights wired in series, one blocked individual can greatly disrupt a small group or team otherwise comprised of individuals who openly display positive attitudes. Therefore, it is often necessary to return to the *individual* energy to change the overall group or *collective* group energy. This may seem obvious, yet it is rarely what managers or leaders have been trained to do.

You probably know of examples when someone addresses a group, a team, or even a whole organization and wants to correct an issue that only applies to a small minority. The intention is usually good. However, it not only demoralizes members of the larger group who know the issue doesn't belong to everyone. It also fails to accomplish the goal of sparking a shift in those to which it applies.

In these situations, it is most effective to work one on one with the individuals who are having (or causing) the issue. You want to help identify the source of their issues in a safe space. This process respects both the energy of the individuals who are at issue and the rest of the team. Quickly and thoughtfully resolving an issue for an individual whose energy negatively affects the group can be essential to regain overall effectiveness.

On the collective level of an organization, it is important to identify and communicate vision, mission, and strategy in a way that all participants of the organization understand. In addition, establishing appropriate goals and objectives that support the vision, mission, and strategy align the collective energies of all who are a part of the company.

How do you create that alignment successfully? By involving all individuals in defining their objectives so they fully embrace them as their own. (None of this is new information, yet many organizations have been known to skip a step or two.) Once you understand the power of aligned collective energy, this sequence takes on a whole new level of importance. Suddenly it becomes apparent that it's not a one-time event but a continuous process to unleash the awesome ability of the human potential inherent in any group of individuals.

In the chapters that follow, you'll find several concepts that support working with the alignment of collective energy. From setting intention to how we communicate, we will look at how to unleash this potential within ourselves and within the collective energy of the organization.

Re-establishing Energy Flow

Faced with individuals whose repeated limiting thought patterns disrupt overall effectiveness, leaders or managers must choose ways to intervene and reestablish energy flow, both individually and collectively. Traditionally, managers would avoid any type of direct intervention in this area; dealing with negative emotion or anything other than the specified process is considered treading on ground reserved for psychologists.

Yet, in the current climate in which not even the illusion of security exists anymore, more people will find themselves up against these areas of resistance. These patterns become more difficult to ignore. And simply getting rid of every individual who is stuck will seem like no one is left to "mind the store."

The good news is that leaders who understand the workings of the subtle energy levels will emerge in organizations. They will know how to intervene with new levels of heart and compassion, aiding those who feel blocked or stuck.

As a leader, if you want to approach problem individuals in new ways, first acknowledge you are dealing with their unconscious thought patterns. This may seem obvious, yet it requires two things: you have taken the time to identify and clear any judgments or blocks you have concerning this individual; and, you have let go of any vested interest in the outcome.

The second point, often stated as "not being attached to the outcome," can be misunderstood as meaning you don't care about the individual who needs this support. The true meaning is *to not have a pre-conceived notion about what the outcome should be for this individual.* Instead, be in an open and centered state, knowing that whatever outcome occurs for the stuck individual is exactly the right outcome for that moment. Solutions arise without any imposed agenda.

Uncovering the Heart of the Issue

Again, take time to identify any limiting decision or judgment you might have about this situation before you intervene. Know that your judgments can limit your own resourcefulness in assisting another. Once your energy is clear and open, then embark on a line of questioning that uncovers the heart of the current issue.

The more specific your questions are, the better. Because limiting thought patterns occur at the subconscious level, the person truly doesn't know a blockage exists, let alone it's source. Therefore, he or she commonly explains away the issue rather than zeroes in on it. Your skill and patience is needed to ask questions that narrow the possibilities.

For instance, the phrase "what specifically" helps narrow the conversation when someone tries to expand it. Use questions like: "What specifically was the cause of the problem? What specifically did you not like about the situation? What specifically was your role in the issue?"

Any time the conversation strays from this line of questioning, always acknowledge the answer but firmly repeat the question so the other person knows you will not back off from discovering the specifics.

Then listen carefully to the answers. When energy is blocked, the person's line of vision is also blocked, so speak to their "blind spot" — the place where others can see the issue yet they cannot. In this place, energy is often distorted and makes little sense to the person whose energy is flowing normally. Yet through this process, you are helping him or her discover the limiting pattern that is distorting or restricting his or her energy.

Again, listen carefully. Even though you think you know the source of the block, you may still be surprised at specific responses. How a person *holds* this information within his or her own mind can be different than how you see it. Understanding and respecting this helps you create greater rapport.

As both you and the individual uncover the specific issue, pursue new options that are good possibilities from the perspective of the other person. Ask, "What will you do differently in the future?"

Sometimes at this point, the individual suddenly sees new possibilities simply because he or she stopped avoiding the specific issue. With this clarity, he or she can connect to new options easily. So help promote these links by simply asking what options are apparent.

Most of the time, this process is all you need to complete the intervention. When this is not the case, be prepared to follow with "what if" questions to explore more possibilities. For example, explore "what specifically" would work (or not work) about each option. All the time, remember the importance of having the individual come up with a solution that will *really* work for him or her.

You can use this process in almost any setting at any time. But understand that, at times, unconscious patterns can run deep or may be complex — having several layers. When this is the case, you may only make a "dent" in an issue that continues to return. When you encounter a problem that runs deep and fear that runs high (in yourself or in others), turn to a trained facilitator or coach who supports people in addressing their issues.

Turning Up the Heat

In today's workplace, the "heat has been turned up" on all leaders and managers. More and more, individuals throughout the organization hold (and challenge) beliefs that no longer work for them. They are, in fact, facing some of their deepest fears and, in doing so, magnetize the appropriate situations around them to work these issues out. This creates the backdrop to help them face their outdated beliefs. *Letting go of control* and *accepting responsibility for their actions* are just two themes people struggle with.

As more people awaken to the thought patterns that have limited them—choosing new thoughts that are open and more positive—the pressure on those who remain in a place of negativity and blame increases. Yet those who embrace their inner awareness not only tap into the infinite source of energy for themselves, they also lead the way for others to do the same.

PROCESS TO SUPPORT OTHERS

1. Before supporting someone else, take a moment to identify any decisions or judgments you may be holding about the situation or person. Use the PROCESS TO IDENTIFY AND CLEAR UNCONSCIOUS THOUGHT PATTERNS.

2. Have the individual start by just explaining the situation. Begin to explore the blind spot. Use questions like, "What specifically caused X?" (X is the issue or situation)

3. As the person identifies specific issues or problems, ask, "What stopped X from happening?" This will help to identify the source of the issue.

4. If the person strays to external issues, respectfully acknowledge this and return to the specific line of questioning.

5. Once the individual discovers the true source of the issue, ask, "What will you do differently in the future?"

Chapter Two
Intention: The Beginning

The scenario is a common one. We begin a new activity with good intentions. We commit to exercising every day or we launch a project, planning to complete it on time and under budget. Yet something happens along the way.

At the beginning when we set out to accomplish something, we have lots of energy. That surge of energy comes from the initial intention, the beginning of any result or outcome one creates in the world.

As described earlier, every thought placed out in the world is, in fact, energy. When individuals launch a new idea or go off in a new direction, they place their intention out there, creating momentum to get the activity started on the right foot.

Every activity we undertake starts with intention. But it's more important to understand that intention also *begins the very reality we create in our environment*. Intention is the core principle behind the concept of visualization. Whether we visualize, set goals and objectives, or simply think about an outcome, we send tremendous energy out to the universe to create what we want. This principle explains why taking time to set clear goals and objectives in our organizations is so important.

Manifesting Results

This chapter is titled "Intention: The Beginning" because intention is the seed. The second part of the equation is commitment, which, like the rain and sun, provides the nourishing energy to manifest whatever is defined by the individual's intention. Only when it is nourished with strong, focused commitment does it produce the desired result. (This is discussed in the next chapter called "Commitment: The Nourishment.")

Turning this equation around, it is also possible to look at the result or outcome and determine what seed or intention was originally planted, just as it is possible to determine what seed was planted by the leaves and fruit the tree bears.

So intention is the blueprint of any new reality an individual desires. Clear intention with solid commitment creates predictably clear results. The opposite is also true–unclear intention (even with strong commitment) generates unclear results.

To better understand this concept, let's look at some basic concepts about creating intention energy.

Owning Intentions

Have you ever said, "It was never my intent to create that result" or "I never intended that to happen?" In such situations, we often find reasons to explain away the result that did occur; we rarely look at the actual intention we put forth to begin with. Instead, we find external explanations for such outcomes: the market was soft, the other department didn't deliver, it was the wrong time, they just didn't understand. However, when individuals begin to understand the role their own energy plays in creating results, a whole new possibility unfolds.

Once open to the awareness of subtle energies, those seeking answers to the question "why this result?" begin to see their own role more clearly. When they trace their steps back to the initial intent they placed out into the world, real answers emerge.

Was the intent pure or was there an ulterior motive at play? Was the intent aligned with the good of the organization, or was a portion of it self-serving? Was the intent simply not aligned to achieve the needed result? Or, was there a deeper unconscious intention or limiting thought pattern that overrode the conscious intention?

Although these questions can be hard to answer truthfully, they are extremely important in identifying why a particular outcome failed to materialize. They're also critical for learning and not repeating the same mistake in the future.

Intentions Versus Goals

You might ask, "Why get all worked up about the concept of intention to begin with?" In the business arena, clear intent is at the heart of any exercise to define goals — whether it be an individual's career goals or goals for an organization. Goals and objectives are forms of defining and documenting intent, thus supporting the concept of placing intention energy out in the world. Whether called a goal, an objective, or an intention, these are essentially the same thing.

In business, most agree that goals, objectives, and follow-through of appropriate action plans *should* create predictable results. Yet "things" can happen to mess up the end result.

By taking time to explore what happened in those cases, you may find that a conflict in the original intent is at the heart of the matter. For instance, many workers have lists of goals and objectives given to them by someone else. As a result, they have no intention (let alone commitment) to adopt these imposed goals. Is it any wonder the anticipated outcome doesn't happen?

A good example happens every time you *tell* (versus ask) someone to do something. Anyone with children *knows* just how well this works! Telling a person to do something assumes that the person is ready and able to create the intention to set forth on the task. However, this rarely is the case.

For instance, telling a child to clean his or her room works when the child has formed a vision of what a clean room will do for him or her. That vision sets the intention; the child most likely will follow through. However, many children do not see any reason to clean their room. The messy room works fine for them! Therefore, the task is not carried out, no matter how many times they are told.

This scenario is not just an issue for parents. The same holds true for any person (child or adult) you try to tell to do something. It certainly plays out in the workplace where it's often assumed that, by just communicating a change, the recipients of the message automatically have their own clear vision to move into action.

If you have been in charge of (or even participated in) rolling out a successful initiative in an organization, you have experienced intention that was properly set in the beginning. When implementation goes smoothly, the change and its impact is clearly communicated and participants determine their roles in carrying out the change. They are given time to internalize what's needed to embrace the new process, system, or concept.

In contrast, implementations that fail often start out on the wrong foot. If participants don't have the opportunity to understand their role in the implementation and the intention is never set, the initiative is doomed at the start. Asking for people to become committed at this point is an up hill battle.

When I implemented several software systems in my early career, understanding intention would have been a great help. User involvement in early stages of the software development became more prevalent in the 1980s—a result of learning that the cost of *not* involving users meant failure. Despite best efforts to design good software, the users of the system always could make or break the final implementation based on their ability to fully utilize it.

The early solutions to solve this problem usually involved demonstrations of system prototypes to help people get a "feel" of the new system. Yet, to support setting proper intention, I now realize that having more dialog would have helped. Taking the time to help the users of a system determine what will be different, including what will change in terms of their processes and workflow, would have ensured a smooth implementation. The software implementers knew some of the answers, but the real answers lie with those who would ultimately use the system.

Aligning Intention for Change

So as we have learned, the only way to have someone *commit* to something is to actively involve that person in creating the original intention. Aligning the organization's intent energy before launching forward with the implementation of the change is the key. This means taking the time up front to make sure the majority of participants understand what will be different as a result of the change and then coming to agreement on the intention (or goals) needed to go forward.

Yet when launching organizational initiatives and communicating goals and/or objectives, leaders often assume everyone will know what to do. Like telling children to clean their room, telling a group the desired outcome doesn't necessarily help people put their own intention (and commitment) energies into action.

The process required to shift this gap is to *communicate* the expected outcome and then *involve* all participants in determining how they would achieve this. Allow them to create their own personal goals that will support this outcome.

Also, have them participate in creating the measurements that will help identify milestones along the path to success. To help enrich the milestones even more, have them explore this question, "What will they need to do differently as a result of the change?" Only when they are involved in creating goals *that they own* will their intention truly be set forth. This, too, is the key for success in manifesting desired outcomes.

Once this process is complete, enormous energy gets released in the direction of the goal(s). That's because the energy of every individual aids in the creation of the vision and the ongoing support of the company's mission.

Intention – Conscious and Unconscious

Goals and objectives are concrete forms of intention at work. Making sure workers set intention by taking ownership of their goals and objectives is imperative for any change process to start on the right foot. Yet, even when employees help define the goal, their own limiting beliefs can unconsciously interfere with their intent (and commitment) to manifest its desired result. That's why managers and leaders require specific skills to probe core issues of intention with workers when appropriate.

Actually, we all deal with intention far more than we realize, for we operate on intentions that are often outside of our conscious awareness. Just about anything we set out to do started with a decision to *do it*. Even when the decision to do or say something *is* in our conscious awareness, a deeper unconscious thought pattern could override the original intent.

A very personal, yet simple, example of a conflicting belief derailing a good intention is reflected in my many attempts to stop drinking coffee. I have tried several attempts to stop drinking coffee, citing that it is not good for my health. Yet each time I stopped "cold turkey," the result lasted for only a couple months. I even tried to change to decaf—but to no avail. Before long, I'd crave a mocha latte or simply a cup of good brewed coffee. After my last attempt failed, I finally asked, "What stops me from being successful in eliminating coffee from my diet?" The answer was so simple! I love the smell and the taste of good coffee, especially on a brisk morning. And decaf just doesn't cut it!

Now, knowing this, I don't waste my time trying to stop drinking coffee. Instead, I let myself thoroughly enjoy it and limit myself to two cups a day. I also realize that if I want to ever eliminate coffee for good, I will need to make a new decision that I truthfully do not like coffee. Until that time, I will enjoy every cup and focus my precious energy on something I'm realistically aligned to change.

This may seem like a trivial example, but stop and think of its implications in organizations. How much energy is being wasted while individuals continue to *try* to change something, only to have their conflicting beliefs sabotage the effort?

Business examples of this scenario can often be found when an organization goes through a major reorganization that involves a change in basic values of the company. This can occur because of accelerated growth, a new style of leadership in a division/department, or a merger or acquisition. I have worked with many employees, managers, and even executives who, finding themselves in a situation where values are changing, have difficulty moving forward with the new objectives of their position. Confused by what is *wrong*, they can become stressed and even depressed in the new situation. Most often, they realize the new position no longer aligns with their original intent for taking the job.

When intent conflicts with a deeper belief or value, feelings of resistance or stress come with it. Common symptoms include these: nothing seems to go right; no matter how much energy is put into creating the result, the outcome does not show up; everything seems like a struggle. Yet struggle is exactly what's happening as the individual keeps trying to override a deeper intention.

Once the conflict is identified, other choices are possible. In the example above, I usually support the individual to find ways to eliminate the conflict, either by changing positions within the organization or, in some cases, by looking for a new position somewhere else. Sometimes it is as simple as telling the truth to a boss who will help shift some of the responsibilities in the existing position. Whatever the solution, the key is to identify the source of the conflict and then resolve it.

So we have looked at how a deeper unconscious belief or intention can conflict with the conscious intent and how this can get in the way of creating the desired outcome. Like any unconscious pattern, this scenario is often easier to see in another person. It can be a real blind spot for the person who, again and again, places good intentions out in the world only to be disappointed by the outcome.

Now let's look at how we can find out what is going on at the source of our intention.

Uncovering True Intent

The benefit of understanding the original intent is that it indicates what result will actually materialize. For instance, if individuals repeatedly get results they say they did not intend, have them explore their *true* intent (which may be quite different from what they thought was their intent).

However, before you look at how to help uncover someone else's intent, become aware of your own intent in facilitating such a process. It is important to understand that if you, as the facilitator, have an ulterior motive or may be out to prove someone wrong, you will not be able to unearth the true intentions of others. What you believe you have discovered may be what you had *presupposed* the problem to be—not necessarily the actual intent. It also will not be possible to create a safe place for individuals who can sense your deeper agenda. So use the five-step process described under PROCESS

TO UNCOVER TRUE INTENT on yourself before working with someone else.

So often, we only ask people "why this result?" It is very important to keep in mind they probably don't know why. It is far more resourceful to ask, "What was the specific result they intended?" With this question, it is possible to help draw out their initial thoughts, guiding them to see how they set the stage to create the result.

In cases when it is difficult for individuals to identify their true intent, there is a high probability you will find an unconscious thought pattern at the source of the issue. Yet without discovering the true intent, they will likely repeat the same thing again. They will obtain results that they do not know how they managed to get or, even worse, they believe they could not possibly deserve.

Often, an individual in this type of pattern will find ways to rationalize the outcome or blame some one or some thing for the unpredictable results. In some cases, the universe may get the blame when people simply refuse to take responsibility for their actions (or thoughts).

Knowledge of identifying intent can help a manager guide an employee on how to create a particular result, or how to make course corrections when things are going in the wrong direction. Here, a manager uses the knowledge of the expected outcome or result to help the individual decide what the intent should be. Helping individuals clarify their intent can bring faster, more reliable results. Clarifying the intent halfway through the process, when things appear off-track, can be extremely helpful to correct a situation.

Process to Uncover True Intent

Here is a step-by-step approach for identifying true intent when the result differs from what an individual believes should be happening.

1. Identify the actual result: First, analyze the result. The idea here is not to ask "why", but to ensure the individual clearly understands what the result is to date. Discuss this thoroughly with the person. Make sure he or she acknowledges that this is, in fact, the result that is occurring.

2. Identify the original intent: Next, simply ask, "When you began this project or activity, what was your original objective or intent?" There are two possible answers you will receive. The first is that the individual will reveal the real intent that has created this result. The sole activity of conducting this inquiry may be all that's needed for the individual to discover he or she got exactly what was intended, even if the person did not believe that when first starting down this path. If this should occur, go immediately to the fifth step.

The other possibility is that the answer will be the intent the individual believes he or she started out with. This may be the intent that the person was originally *told* he or she needed to have (in other words, the *right* answer). It is possible you may immediately understand the gap or conflict that exists between the person's stated intent and the *real* intent. Be aware that, at this point of the inquiry, this individual believes this is his or her *true* intent. *Do not* try to alter the person's beliefs or convince the individual that he or she is *wrong*, for this would clearly jeopardize the trust and rapport you want to build. Honor the person's honesty in sharing his or her *perceived* intent with you. That will set the stage to help get you through the next step.

Give plenty of space when asking this question. In delving into the original intent, individuals could unearth some things they were not really clear on when they set the intention in motion. This is exactly the outcome you want to achieve: *facilitating a process that helps people discover for themselves what went wrong or what is at the source of the conflict in their intention.* This way, they can determine what actions they need to take to correct the process in the future. Since they participate in the solution it is the best way to obtain true commitment to a change, and it requires little personal energy to facilitate the change. Best of all it will have a high probability of success.

3. Identify the expected result: This step helps an individual discover his or her true intent. To begin with, ask, "What result did you expect to achieve based on your stated intent?" The individual will most likely describe the result you both wanted in the first place. Then ask, "How did you originally expect to attain that result?" This will move the person back to some of the internal thoughts he or she went through in planning the initial process.

Take good notes, for you will likely uncover pieces of the puzzle to help you understand the original intent. Whenever possible, ask what the individual intended for each small step on the path leading to the end result. As you move through this questioning, you will help the person uncover steps leading to this point in time. If the questioning goes well, the person is likely to quickly discover any problems in his or her original intent. When this occurs, acknowledge the person for having the courage and patience to discover the true intent, and then go to directly to the fifth step.

4. Identify what prevented the outcome: This step continues to help the individual uncover his or her deeper intent or conflicting beliefs that altered the outcome. Ask, "What do you believe stopped you from achieving your desired results?" The person may answer with only problems. If so, respectfully acknowledge those and continue to probe. You can repeat the "What stopped you (or the team)?" question as the person identifies each external issue. With patience, you are supporting the person in identifying the real issue. If, after

45

several unsuccessful attempts to encourage discovery of the person's own intent, use a "what if" or "is it possible" statement followed by the statement of the intent you believe you have uncovered by your questioning. Once the individual sees his or her true intent, move to the fifth and final step.

5. Identify actions to close the gap: Ask, "What would you do differently to create the desired objectives or results?" This helps the person determine how to reset his or her intent. You might think this step would be easy, especially once the individual understands the difference between what he or she thought was the intent and the unconscious intent that was really driving the outcome. However, the degree of ease in this step is directly proportional to the degree of ease it took for the individual to discover the discrepancy.

If the person discovered the true intent when asked the first questions, you can be assured the correction will be simple and swift. However, if you had to resort to asking a "what if" question, you may find the individual had problems owning the intent or aligning the intent to achieve the desired result. At this point, you will probably experience resistance. Once again, this signifies an unconscious thought pattern at work, creating a blind spot or a reality the individual would rather keep hidden. If the individual has a strong belief that people and/or situations show up as strictly wrong or right, this person may be up against admitting that he or she is *wrong* even though that is not your intent.

This thought pattern may be a basic limiting belief about the person and may affect his or her ability to accomplish a particular task or project. For example, the person may doubt he or she can really do this, or the person may strongly disbelieve either in the activity he or she has been chartered to do, or in the manner to be carried out. One example is asking an individual with strong perfectionist tendencies to accomplish an activity in a time frame he or she doesn't believe

46

is realistic or doesn't want to face. Asking this would conflict with the intended "perfect" result.

These types of issues will take more probing and well-thought-out negotiations to reset the intent to a place that will obtain the result. Although this may seem like a lot of effort, the benefit is alignment and the knowledge that the outcome will be achieved.

Remember, in going through this process, you may discover important insights regarding *your own intent* for accomplishing this task. For instance, this could happen when individuals admit they do not believe a specific task can be accomplished in a particular time frame. This might be part of a perfectionist issue for the individual; however, it also might bring up issues *for you,* too. Facing this possibility can be the difference between success and failure as it relates to business.

There will be times when it will not be possible to get people past the conflicts or unconscious thought patterns that are overriding their intent. This happens most frequently when someone has a major limiting belief concerning the issue of responsibility. Clearly, individuals who refuse to take responsibility for their actions will have major difficulty in believing their intent has anything to do with an outcome. Usually an individual with this type of pattern will blame others for the result that has manifested.

When encountering individuals dealing with a major limiting belief around responsibility, remember they truly do not believe they have any power to change the intent. Or perhaps they do not believe their own intent has any power to influence, let alone manifest, results. Most importantly, they may not be ready to look at this belief at this time.

If, after several attempts to connect them to this issue, they cannot understand it, assess how critical their role is for the overall result you are managing. If they are in a crucial role, it may be best (for both the individual and their colleagues) to move them to a place where they follow others who can lead the effort.

Individuals with extreme issues concerning responsibility need well-defined boundaries. Ironically, it is often their desire to expand beyond those boundaries that finally forces them to re-evaluate what holds them back. Only at this point of understanding can they be ready to identify what is at the source of their responsibility issues and make a new decision to increase their effectiveness. Then they can move into a place of taking personal responsibility for their thoughts, their actions, and ultimately for what they manifest in the world.

PROCESS TO UNCOVER TRUE INTENT

1. **Identify the actual or current result. Reach agreement that this is what occurred.**

2. **Ask, "When you began this project or activity, what was your original objective or intent?"** *If the person identifies the true intent that created the result, go to Step 5.*

3. **Ask, "Based on your original objective or intent, what result did you expect to achieve?"** *Most likely, they will identify the same result that you both wanted in the beginning.*

4. **Ask, "What do you believe stopped you (or the team) from achieving this objective?"** *Continue to explore this fully until the true intent or conflicting belief is identified.*

5. **Ask, "What will you do differently to achieve the intended outcome?"**

Uncovering Personal Intent

As mentioned before, looking at personal intent is an important part of managing your energy. Although it may seem a difficult exercise at times, a wise leader can come to some important understandings about his or her own intentions by fully accepting the results created. This is true, even though the result may not be what was expected. They need to look introspectively for the actual intent that initiated those results. Owning their role in creating a given outcome can be a powerful growth experience. It is also an excellent way to make powerful course corrections on the path to creating a desired organization.

Often the best way to diagnose your own true source of intention energy is to watch for a pattern that repeats, especially those that pertain to a particular result (or no result, as the case may be). This real clue can start you on a path to resolution.

Like all energy blockages, these types of patterns can drain energy significantly, especially if they reflect a pattern you constantly repeat in short intervals. From the energy perspective, one can literally expend enormous personal energy to create an intention and on-going commitment energy continually without achieving the desired result. Here again, the deeper unconscious intent conflicts with the desired outcome, thus sabotaging the results. The PROCESS TO UNCOVER TRUE INTENT can also be used to discover your own intentions when the results are not what you originally expected.

Intent and Collective Energy

Understanding the role intent plays in creating a result on an individual level is key to understanding how intent works in the bigger picture of group dynamics. Using this knowledge, a leader or manager can expand the principles to be used in the collective energy of the organization.

Creating and aligning collective intent is an important function for a leader or manager of any organization. There are two main steps to accomplish this. First, the leader must be clear about his or her personal intent and the intent for the organization. This is the primary function of the vision statement. Taking time to truly define the vision (and mission) helps crystallize this first in the minds of those leading the organization, for it's there that the initial intention energy is set.

Second, the vision must be communicated and embraced by all individuals within the organization to become reality. Many leaders fail in this area, for they believe they have communicated the message when, in fact, it was not received. The result of unfocused energy and confused priorities is often proof that the message did not get through.

Communicating intent to create a mass result requires far more than a memo or a one-time presentation to the staff. It entails repeated communications using various means to get the message across: conversations at multiple levels, setting an example of the message, aligning the environment to support the message. Ideally, everything the individuals in the company encounter should reinforce the vision.

The next challenge is to engage the people of the organization in determining what this means for each of them. What part does each of them play in creating the results? Identifying and sharing success stories of employees demonstrating their understanding of the vision provides a beacon to help further align the intent.

Most people fail to see the direct and powerful connection between their intent and the results they create in their world. Yet our thoughts are shaping the world around us whether we are aware of it or not. Realizing the critical part that each and every person contributes in setting intention to reach company goals could make a profound difference in the way corporations set goals and objectives within their boundaries.

When each person in the organization begins to radiate the same intent, incredible amounts of energy are released, creating momentum that few companies have had the privilege to experience.

Chapter Three
Commitment: The Nourishment

Commitment is the foundation on which so many things are built. In the business arena, commitment is one of those things that "you know it when you have it"—and it is painfully obvious when you don't!

Much is written today about the need for leaders to be committed to initiatives like quality, empowerment, and customer satisfaction—not to mention the standard areas of profit and growth. Commitment is a key factor in driving change in an organization. The word is used frequently, yet few understand its meaning and, most importantly, few know how to actually obtain it.

As noted in the previous chapter on intent, commitment is the other half of the equation to create or manifest results in the world. With all the emphasis on results in business today, understanding the underlying components that make up any result is an important priority.

The Critical Ingredient

Although commitment is described as the key ingredient in implementing change, without understanding that *intention precedes commitment* and how it works in relation with commitment, one doesn't see the whole picture. This is critical to remember when rolling out a new program. Asking people to become committed to something in which they may not *intend* to participate is a sure road to failure.

Many people mouth the words of commitment without being truly committed. So you may observe at times an individual committed on an intellectual level yet not demonstrating commitment in action. In these situations, the individual may have doubts about the outcome. Doubt inhibits or cancels the intellectual or mental level of commitment. So for commitment to be a key factor for moving forward, commitment must be aligned both mentally and physically. This alignment is called "walking the talk." That's when people truly model whatever they are committed to.

Commitment is Focused Energy

Leaders in organizations are challenged to know where to focus energy — in other words, to *where* and *what* do they place their commitment. Often the message is not clear regarding the organization's top priorities. Worse yet is the organization where the verbal message is clear, yet the realities that the employees are facing clearly conflict with the priority that has been handed down from the top.

What is most disheartening about the last scenario is that the individuals expend an enormous amount of commitment energy that is literally being wasted. The challenge for leaders and managers is aligning the flow of energy so that it can be channeled into a common direction that moves the organization toward a desired result.

Commitment is simply focused energy. When an individual commits to some cause, he or she has already put forth energy in the form of an aligned intention. The success of this commitment is determined by the amount of energy that continues to be focused on this particular cause. Unfortunately, many things can disrupt this flow of commitment energy.

Three Barriers to Commitment

To better understand how commitment energy works, it is helpful to start by understanding what barriers get in the way of commitment. There are three main barriers that inhibit commitment. All three produce the same outward result: a lack of commitment. Therefore, when trying to correct a situation in which failed commitment is suspected, it is important to identify which of these barriers is active. Diagnosing the underlying reasons for the failed commitment will help to determine what action is needed to get a group or team back on track—achieving the desired result. This is true whether the commitment failure is your own or belongs to someone within the team you are counting on for support.

1. Intention was never created: This type of commitment failure happens at the beginning when people declare their intentions. They *say* they are committed because it's the *correct* thing to do; however, they don't actually place their intentions out in the world, so commitment never begins.

Most problems with commitment are blamed on this when, in reality, it is rarely the cause of failed commitment. For instance, have you ever been accused of not being committed to something when you feel strongly that you are? You probably had full intentions of accomplishing or backing whatever it was that you were asked to do; however, something happened to the ongoing commitment energy. Chances are one of the following two barriers prevailed.

2. Limiting thought patterns: This is similar to intentions that are derailed by underlying beliefs. Limiting thought patterns such as doubt or conflicting beliefs could sabotage commitment. Intention gets created but, over time, doubt grows until the commitment gets totally canceled out. This happens when one's underlying beliefs have not been changed to accommodate a new intention. Or it happens when more information comes in that conflicts with what one is committing to.

Many years ago, I was working with a computer operations team for a medium-sized manufacturing firm. I was brought in to facilitate a session with a manager's direct reports. The intent was to renew the vision and identify associated changes in their strategy for the next couple of years.

This team had been fairly successful in meeting the defined service requirements in the last few years. However, the director knew that recent changes in upper management were going to raise the bar in what was expected of his team so he wanted to get ahead of the curve. Over the previous four years, he had built a team of employees who took service seriously. They had been through several challenges, so they regarded this as just another one along the way. Yet, this time something was holding his team back.

When researching the situation, I thought he had done all the right things to prepare his team. They had gone through their usual year-end planning process when he discussed the challenges they were facing. He had his team brainstorm solutions and identify best actions, along with setting goals and objectives. The team defined milestones to measure progress; each team member seemed "psyched" to implement them. Yet, in the few months that followed, the enthusiasm had waned and target dates were slipping. He had questioned key people, even did some roundtable discussions with different people in his organization. Yet, he couldn't get a definitive answer on what was at the core of the issue. Listening to all of this, I realized that an issue of intention or commitment might be at the source, and a deeper issue needed to be revealed.

On the day of the actual team session, I began by focusing the group on the vision (or group intention). This first step went smoothly. Team members knew where they wanted to go and were definitely aligned. The director had done a good job helping them set their intention. However, when we got to the implementation strategy, I could feel areas of doubt enter into the conversation. We had been reconfirming actions committed to by the group months before. Now, when it was required to restate its course of action, people hesitated to commit to a date. Feeling the resistance, I asked, "What is stopping you from clearly committing to these timeframes?"

Total silence filled the room. Finally, one brave soul looked around and slowly began to speak. "I suppose someone has to tell the truth about this. One of us has obtained some credible information that the new management is planning to outsource us as early as next year. We know this information wasn't for us to hear, but I know I am wondering if I should be spending my time updating my résumé."

With the entire team facing extinction as a possible future, no wonder the commitment to the agreed-upon plan kept eroding. That was the factor derailing the commitment energy. The director knew that outsourcing was a possibility, but being a part of the conversations with upper management, he had a different perspective. That is exactly why he set out to raise the bar. He knew that if his group could meet the higher service levels, its future would be solid. But he did not communicate the outsourcing possibility because it was confidential and because he knew his team could rise to the challenge. Now, putting this information out on the table, the group could clear the doubt and recommit to the level of success they were capable of achieving.

This example shows how doubt can be a powerful force that disrupts commitment energy. It also shows how doubt can set up. The belief that the team members did not have a future with this organization set up doubt when they started to engage in the agreed-upon implementation. This case further demonstrates the importance of asking, "What stops you from doing this?" The director realized he had asked questions on what could be improved, thinking perhaps *he* had done something wrong. However, he never directly asked what barrier was keeping them from carrying out the actions they had committed to originally.

3. Outdated commitments: The third area of failed commitment happens most commonly in business and leads to the most stress. This occurs when new commitments are made that overlap or even override the original commitment. Changing commitments is not a bad thing. But when it occurs, people do not usually delete the old commitment (and the original intent) from their "to do" lists. As a result, they feel overextended, burdened, and, of course, stressed. The simple act of canceling out the old commitment—recognizing it is no longer active—frees up enormous amounts of energy for any new commitment to take hold.

BARRIERS TO OBTAINING COMMITMENT

1. **Intention was never created in the first place, so there's nothing to commit to.**

2. **Limiting thought patterns such as doubt or a conflicting belief sabotages or overrides the commitment.**

3. **Conflicting priorities or old, outdated commitments inhibit the new commitment.**

Maintaining Commitment

Those who recognize the need to maintain focus on what is important can help create fertile ground for commitment energy to continue. This facilitates a speedy path to the desired result. Yet, in this day and age, that is no small task! Overload of responsibilities and conflicting priorities take a major toll on achieving successful results in today's hectic business environment. Doing more with less has become a way of life for many in the workplace. People find they have little time to think or plan the next action, let alone plan several steps down the path.

In one company, I interviewed managers whose jobs were restructured as a result of a major downsizing. This particular level of manager now had responsibility for two distinct functions that had been handled by two people before. Some managers didn't make it; overwhelmed by the stress, they left for other positions. Those who successfully rose to the challenge did so by assessing priorities quickly, focusing on only those that were most important. In addition, they guided their work groups to do the same.

The challenge for managers and leaders in these and similar situations is to manage priorities in a new way. They not only must constantly be prioritizing, they must also learn to de-prioritize, or in more radical situations, "de-implement" goals and objectives that no longer apply. This requires first the fortitude to *stop,* and then to take time to review the active goals or initiatives to assure they still make sense. Once goals are identified that no longer fit the new scenario, clearly communicating them to those affected frees up precious collective energy.

Aligning Intention and Commitment for Change

As we learned in the chapter on intention, taking precious time to discuss, "What does this change mean to us?" can be the difference between getting slow, confused, mixed results and a successful implementation that aligns the collective energy to manifest the desired results. It takes a fairly simple frame of questioning to help a group assimilate what this change means to them. Now that we understand both intention and commitment, let's look at the whole process.

1. Describe the change: Begin this process by describing the change (to the best of your ability), including the *reason* the change is taking place. This last point—communicating the reason for the change—is extremely important, yet it is often forgotten when rolling out a new initiative or communicating a change in strategy. Understanding the "why" behind something sets the foundation for others to make meaning of the change.

To clearly communicate the actual change, first speak to "what's new" and then describe, "what's over" as a result of this change. As previously noted, identifying what no longer applies frees up precious energy. Past objectives, initiatives, and priorities that end as a result of the change are not always obvious to the employees. And the managers rolling out the change don't often think through what no longer applies, either. That leaves employees to guess or figure it out over time. Again, this results in a significant waste of collective energy. To avoid this, managers who take time to identify the areas that are complete can better help their organization implement the change quickly.

2. Allow participants to identify what the change means to them: After stating the situation, have employees brainstorm these questions: What do they need to *start* doing, *continue* doing, and *stop* doing? If you have multiple functional areas present, have employees break into their own area of responsibility to complete the exercise. These questions guide staff members to take the information presented by the manager to a deeper level of understanding. In turn, sharing their insights helps the manager better understand where more clarity may be needed.

3. Share the findings: To gain insight, complete this step by having individual groups share what they discovered. Much of the discussion may not be a surprise to you. Yet often this exercise brings to light some areas that need further discussion. Again, this provides an excellent opportunity to make any course corrections right up front before the change is implemented. Either way, you have assisted in aligning the collective energy of the group. By allowing all individuals to identify what they must do differently and then having them share insights, implementing the change is much more likely to start off in the right direction.

ALIGNING INTENTION AND COMMITMENT FOR CHANGE

1. Describe the change to the participants, include: The reason the change is taking place; "What is new?" as a result of this change; and, "What is over?" because of this change.

2. Have the participants meet in functional groups to brainstorm: What do they need to *start* doing; *continue* doing; and, *stop* doing?

3. Have the each group share their findings with the larger group.

This process not only ensures that the intent is aligned; it lays the foundation for commitment to be focused on manifesting the desired results. Managing the ongoing commitment energy becomes a matter of focus and managing priorities.

Commitment and Going with the Flow

It is important to understand that, like intent, commitment must be aligned with universal principle if one is truly to manifest results in the world. This is an important point, for many expend enormous amounts of energy being committed to things that flow against basic principles. This could be compared to trying to row a boat upstream. You may have clear intent and be very committed to getting to a destination located upstream, but paddling a boat in heavy downstream current will not likely get you to your intended destination. Some other mode of transportation, such as walking or driving along the river's edge, will work much better because these don't go against the natural flow of universal energies.

Building on this concept, it is often helpful to notice what seems to be difficult. When something you are committed to feels difficult, it is a good sign that you may be going (or rowing) "against the flow." Just the simple act of acknowledging this possibility will be enough to change the energy flow. At the moment one considers this, resistance stops, stress releases, and new options suddenly open for consideration.

This could be compared to the moment an individual realizes he or she is rowing against the current. The moment this person pulls the paddle from the water, the resistance caused by the energy expended on rowing ceases. Also, at the same moment, the boat will begin to move in the opposite direction, indicating the natural flow of the energy at work.

It may seem silly to consider rowing a boat upstream because one can obviously see the water flowing in the opposite direction. However, for many people, this example is exactly what they undertake every day of their lives. They refuse to pay attention to the natural forces at work in the world around them.

In some cases, analyzing whether the commitment energy aligns with the natural forces may point out that the original intent was faulty. In these situations, it is imperative to re-look at the goal or objective and determine if an appropriate course correction is warranted. However, the opposite can also occur. Since commitment is the energy expended to actually manifest the intent, one can initiate intent that is truly aligned with universal principle, and then try to create it in a way that goes against the flow. Using the example above, there is nothing wrong with the intention of getting to a destination upstream; however, to be committed to doing so by rowboat is a problem.

This example illustrates just how important it is for individuals—especially the leaders of organizations—to understand *how* and *on what* they expend commitment energy. When a corporation's commitment energy is truly aligned in a common direction, extraordinary results happen.

Understanding the importance that both intent and commitment energy play in creating the cherished end results, leaders of tomorrow are challenged to recognize their responsibility in aligning both the intent and commitment of the collective energy of the individuals who make up their organizations.

Chapter Four
Integrity: The Journey to Wholeness

Integrity is a character trait we value in people we look up to, whether it is our parent or boss. The question is, "What do we define as integrity?" When asked, the typical answer comes back as someone who is honest, truthful, or trustworthy. The person may be described as having character. This definition is fairly consistent with texts on leadership whose descriptions of integrity also include the following characteristics: ethical, consistent (they follow through and do what they say they are going to do), and congruent, where thought, word, and action are aligned (often expressed as "walking your talk").

Based on this definition, having integrity is a tall order for anyone to model. Unfortunately, we are often disappointed by the lack of integrity in those we expect to have the most.

Looking for Integrity

But perhaps we have been looking for integrity in "all the wrong places!" Before we can find it in someone else, we must secure it within ourselves. This means taking a hard look within the self, identifying areas in which we aren't always consistent or "show up" for those around us.

Integrity is not something we find "out there." Instead it is found as one makes the journey within to know one's own self. It also is not something that can be taught, for it is not a skill. Instead, integrity is the result of an individual's inner work, coming to terms with who he or she really is.

This is *real* honesty, for it takes courage to know all sides of one's *true* self—both the side that shines light into the world and the dark side where energies may yet be blocked.

As implied by this chapter's title "Integrity: The Journey To Wholeness," it is this inner search that provides an opening to our deepest levels of awareness and authenticity. It is through this inner journey that we begin to express integrity to the world.

Integrity has three distinct facets that support this journey to wholeness—(1) quieting one's mind, (2) learning to be centered in the present moment, and (3) identifying and clearing unconscious thought patterns that cause emotional blockages. Focusing on these three areas provides the roadmap to open to one's inner awareness. Resulting discoveries are unique for each individual.

Quieting the Mind

The very thought of quieting the mind just doesn't sound logical when used in a business context. In our results-driven world of work, quieting the mind implies a shutdown of the mental process—hardly something one would expect to get paid to do. Yet it is exactly this process that can increase our personal productivity, increase our creativity, and reduce the stress we have become so accustomed to in our fast-changing environment.

Other cultures around the world, specifically those in the Far East, know the power that a quiet mind brings. In China, the workday begins with Tai Chi, a form of meditation in movement that not only stills and focuses the mind, it aids in being in the present moment. Workers go to their place of employment in this state of centeredness. They start their days refreshed and focused — a far cry from how the typical business day starts in the West.

We usually think of meditation when the topic of quieting the mind is brought up. Certainly meditation can effectively empty the mind and calm the body. A regular practice of deep meditation also helps *maintain* a quiet mind. Yet, one does not need to go to a mountaintop and sit in deep meditation for an extended period of time to gain the benefit of a quiet mind. We can still our minds easily through techniques that require little time and can be done virtually anywhere.

First of all, it is important to understand the deep connection between our breath and our thoughts. When the mind races with information, breathing is usually rapid and quite shallow, with only the upper part of the lungs being used. When the mind is quiet, the breath slows down with all lung capacity in use. Therefore, one can quiet the mind by becoming aware of one's breathing. Conversely, slowing and deepening the breath will begin the process of quieting the mind.

Secondly, the mind can only focus on one thing. When our minds try to juggle a myriad of details, we are doing just that — quickly running our mind from detail to detail or issue to issue. In this mode, focus eludes us. But most importantly, being in this mode prevents us from accessing the intuitive side of the brain—the very resource that could bring creative breakthrough into action.

Due to this connection between the breath and the mind, most exercises to quiet the mind begin by focusing on the breath. In coaching individuals on bringing this practice into their daily routine, I found an exercise (PROCESS TO CENTER THE BODY) to use with people who have difficulty. It helps focus the mind first, then concentrate on the breath. Here's how I discovered this technique.

For several years, my job required me to travel almost every week. I was a director of human resources working with management teams on anything from development to resolution of major personnel issues. Many weeks, I landed in a different city every other day. Needless to say, a fair amount of stress came with this position. In addition, I carried my office with me in my briefcase, making it tough to get a break from work. So I learned to meditate in hotel rooms and quiet my mind "on the fly" — in airports, airplanes, and office conference rooms. This simple exercise kept me sane. You may do it sitting or standing. If you are sitting, take a moment to uncross your legs and place your feet on the floor.

Exercise to Quiet the Mind

Begin by choosing any object in your line of sight. Concentrate on this object, gazing at it like you have never seen it before. Notice the colors, the texture, and the shape. Focus on the object, noticing as much detail as possible. As you concentrate on one thing, you'll notice that your breath automatically slows down and deepens. This process stops your mind from wandering.

Now move your awareness to the soles of your feet. Notice how they feel, how they make contact with the earth. Take a moment to appreciate how they support you. Bringing your awareness to your feet helps bring your conscious awareness to your body. This not only aids in quieting your mind, it also begins the process of centering your body.

After several moments of focusing on your feet, slowly move your awareness to your breath. By now it will have slowed substantially from when you began. Focus only on the breath. Note how easily the air moves in and out with each inhalation and exhalation. Again, take a moment to appreciate how this nourishes and supports you. Although we take it for granted, breathing is one of the main ways we bring vital energy into our bodies.

The real key to sustaining this state is to repeat this process throughout your day. By building in just a few moments to stop and focus your attention, you will regularly experience the enormous benefit that a quiet mind can give. You can start in the morning either before leaving home or as soon as you arrive in the office. If you have a challenging commute to the office, both times are recommended. Taking a few minutes before starting out can make the commute go more smoothly, and spending a few moments upon arrival can clear any stress created by the drive into work.

PROCESS TO QUIET THE MIND

1. **Choose any object to concentrate on. Gaze at it like you have never seen it before, noticing every detail.**

2. **Move your awareness to the soles of your feet. Notice how they feel. Continue this focus for several moments.**

3. **Move your awareness to your breath. Notice how easily the air moves in and out with each inhalation and exhalation. Take a moment to appreciate how this nourishes you.**

Centering the Body

Being centered links closely with quieting the mind. The main distinction is that quieting the mind focuses on the energy generated by one's thoughts. Being centered focuses on the energetic state of the body.

Like quieting the mind, slowing the breath is a pre-requisite of becoming centered. As it aids the mind to clear, this action also nourishes and calms the entire body. This is why slowing and deepening the breath relieves stress quickly.

So, quieting of the mind can lead to centering of the body and being in the present moment. Our hectic lifestyles have all but disconnected us to the important consciousness stored in our bodies. We spend much more time in a state of mental activity than in a place where we become in tune with our bodies. That's why quieting the mind helps to get "in touch" with our inner awareness.

With practice, we learn that the body holds much awareness that we may be unaware of. Bringing it to a place of center opens the door to the innate intelligence residing there. This is where we store much of the information concerning one's personal blockages. Therefore, like the deep connection between breath and thoughts, there is a deep connection between being centered and clearing one's own limiting patterns. Taking time to center the body reveals where deep emotional blocks are stored. In turn, clearing these blocks helps the body remain in a centered state.

It is difficult to describe the concept of being centered because it resides in the realm of feeling. One needs to *feel* what it is like to be centered, not discuss it intellectually. Here, I am restricted to written words on the page and must make the most of these restraints.

Achieving a Centered State

To begin to tap into the *feeling* of being centered, take a moment out of your day, preferably at its beginning. Recharge at some point in the mid-day and again before you leave work. Simply close your office door if you can and take a moment for silence. If you are in a private space, close your eyes. If you are in an area where this may not be comfortable, do the exercise explained earlier. That is, find an object in your line of sight that you can comfortably gaze on.

PROCESS TO CENTER THE BODY

1. If possible, create a space where you won't be interrupted. Close your eyes.

2. Focus on your breath, taking deep, slow breaths from the bottom of your lungs.

3. Notice any place where your body is tight or feels restricted. Ask that part of your body to relax, breathing into that specific spot until the tightness dissolves.

4. Continue to scan for areas of tightness, repeating Step 3.

You may notice your breathing becoming shallow as concerns mount. When that happens, take time to calm yourself, releasing whatever stress or issues you carry in your mind. Focus on your breath, taking deep and slow breaths and filling your lungs from the bottom. Slowing and deepening the breath can immediately open any constricted energy flow in the body.

As you focus on your breath, notice any place where your body feels tight or restricted. Ask that part of your body to relax. Imagine you are breathing life into that specific spot. Notice how the body responds as tightness begins to dissolve. Continue to scan it for any areas that feel tight. At each point, focus your breath on that spot until it relaxes. Continue this process for at least ten minutes or as long as you need to completely relax. Even five minutes can be revitalizing and help you deal with whatever comes your way.

The more you practice being centered, the more you will notice a substantial reduction in the time it takes between realizing your stress level is high and taking a moment to do this exercise. Eventually, you will be able to evoke this state quickly even when in a difficult situation. Once centered with your energy flowing fully, you will find yourself more resourceful and more able to deal with the situation at hand.

Another approach to centering the body is to think of a time when you felt totally calm, a feeling of being at peace with yourself. Perhaps it was when you were a child without a care in the world or when you were on vacation looking at a sunset, walking on a beach. Settle on a time when your mind was empty of the concerns of daily living.

Recall as many details as you can about this experience with your whole body. Remember the sights, the sounds, and most importantly, the feelings you experienced. Once fully centered in the experience, bring this feeling of centeredness into the present moment.

ANOTHER PROCESS TO CENTER THE BODY

1. Think of a time when you felt totally calm and at peace with yourself.

2. Recall as many details as you can, remembering the sights, sounds, and feelings of this experience.

3. Once centered in the experience, bring the feeling of this experience to the present moment.

The more you begin to know this feeling, the more you will want to evoke this condition—for the mind-body responds favorably to it. You will begin to experience a whole new level of confidence because, in this state, you tap into the universal source of energy rather than simply your own source of personal energy.

Accessing the Present Moment

Once you feel centered, take a moment to locate your awareness. This may at first sound like a strange request, but it is actually quite important. Worrying about tomorrow or fretting over the past are small examples of awareness in some place and time other than the present.

You can only create your future by what you accomplish in the present moment. The past can either continue to control you or you can choose to release it in the present moment. When releasing the past seems impossible, an active unconscious thought pattern may be at the source of the matter. Strategies used to push the past away are just that—strategies—which simply put off dealing with the inevitable. Trying to "stuff" the past creates an ongoing energy drain and can eventually lead to "dis-ease" in the body.

How does all this relate to the workplace? Mastering a centered state (including quieting the mind) is key to relieving stress in the workplace. When the mind and body are stressed, breathing is shallow and restricted. This creates an endless cycle that limits one's mental resources.

Once the mind has slowed down and the energy in the body is aligned, you can more easily choose where to place your awareness. In addition, calming the mind and centering the body provide focus, clarity, and access to one's natural creative abilities. These are the exact resources one needs most in times of enormous pressure.

I have found that I can achieve far more when in this state. It would seem that this is a state of non-action; however, nothing is further from the truth. A quiet mind and centered state of being allows you to focus on the present—the only place where change can truly happen.

In addition, being in the present is a critical pre-requisite to *truly* listening—a skill often talked about but very difficult to put into practice. This ability to be fully present allows you to listen deeply to what another person is saying. Trying to listen when your mind goes in many directions and your body's energy is scattered doesn't work. When they are in a centered state, deep listening takes very little effort. It is just a matter of focus.

Clearing Energy Blockages

The concepts of energy blockages and how to clear them were introduced in the first chapter, "Energy: The Source." In relationship to integrity, it is important to focus more deeply on just how our own limiting thoughts hold us in undesired patterns. These patterns affect both our personal lives and our ability to make a difference in the world.

Blockages inhibit us from being in integrity and "walking our talk." Unfortunately, these limiting patterns are often visible only to others. They take the form of blind spots for the individual who owns them.

Once again, this inner journey supports the discovery and release of these areas of energy drain. Along with the obvious consequences of not dealing with these limiting thoughts and beliefs, you continue to draw people and experiences into your life (which includes your routines at work) that provide opportunities to fully experience your blockages. This means any reaction—anger, resentment, fear, anxiety, blame, and more—that seems to result from an external source is really your gateway to a blocked area. You can always find its true source in the self.

No matter what your role or rank within an organization, the people who surround you provide ample interactions to see inside your inner self. The key here is to shift your perception from looking for the external cause of your reaction to looking for the trigger or block within. This simple shift in perception can change your whole perspective on what happens at your place of employment.

Shifting Perceptions

For myself, this profound shift in perception has proven to be invaluable. Known as a top achiever in many of my corporate positions, I always knew how to get things accomplished. I never thought of myself as one who looked outside of me for reasons why something didn't happen. I saw shouldering responsibility as all part of my role. Yet, an experience that happened just as my awareness was beginning to open helped me understand how much my own energy (and blockages) controlled my destiny at work.

On a fast track within a large organization, I had been promoted to a senior management position in a division of the company that was new to me. I was a part of a team of seven peers reporting to a vice president. I was truly excited with the challenges the position presented me and started off with total enthusiasm.

However, not far into the mission, I found myself stopped at every turn. This environment lacked vision and direction; commitment was non-existent. People would say one thing and do another as a basic mode of operating. Backstabbing among my peers and our leader happened regularly. Over time, I found myself totally drained from working with this group. I tried to stay afloat in the midst of a political nightmare that wouldn't go away.

I desperately wanted to leave this situation, yet I couldn't seem to bring myself to look for another job. The company resided in an area where few other employment options existed. Because of this, I knew I had to relocate to another area of the country. That made a career move all that much more difficult.

Deep inside, I knew something had to give. I got to a point where it took every ounce of my own personal energy to face each day. I felt completely drained and trapped. My effectiveness at work faltered — something that scared me even more.

Totally exhausted and discouraged, I got away on an extended weekend retreat. While on this retreat, I went into a deep meditation. I asked for guidance about what I should do and where I should go. I could not understand why I was working with this dysfunctional group of people and, most importantly, why I couldn't seem to just get up and leave.

At first, when the answer came back to me, I didn't want to believe it. Yet I knew the first insight was usually the true answer. Simply and directly I heard, "When you release your judgment of these people, all that you seek will be revealed to you." I was astounded! I hadn't realized the amount of judgment I held concerning this group. And, even if all opinions were true, in my own mind I had total justification for my judgments from several credible sources in other parts of the company.

Then, in what seemed like a flash, I began to "see the light" in each one of my peers, including my boss. I suddenly realized that each person was working through emotional blocks created in his or her own past. Yet, I had labeled them "dysfunctional," judging that they were truly wrong and not in integrity. This caused me to feel stuck. I suddenly understood that, on a deep level, they were each doing the best they could.

On Monday, I returned to work a different human being. Looking at this group with new eyes, the entire team changed overnight. But of course, it was not them…it was me who had changed. Almost immediately, they responded to me differently, with more interest and respect. Within two months of this revelation, I received the answer to my questions. I'd found a location where I wanted to live and landed my next position. Three months later, I headed across the country toward my new life. Those last five months of my employment with this group were the best months I had in my four years with the company. I felt happier and much lighter. I also accomplished a great deal. What was most remarkable was the respect I received from my boss and my peers. I left on the best of terms.

At the time, I didn't understand the full impact of this shift. However, knowing the powerful hold that blocked energy has, I now realize that by going within and clearing my judgments, I create safe space for others to interact with me. This is so important, for we often think that our thoughts do not impact others. The fact is, our thoughts are powerful projections of energy that not only affect people we interact with every day, they affect the results we create in the world.

In clearing my judgments, I became more open. My level of authenticity increased as my thoughts — now safe to express — aligned with my words and my actions.

Integrity: The Benefits

So it is that integrity continues to grow as one continues on a journey to wholeness. The more one quiets the mind, centers the body, and remains committed to the clearing of their own limiting patterns, the more alignment occurs. The mind, body, and spirit come into a natural state of alignment as the journey continues. As mentioned earlier, this leads to a state of greater authenticity in which people naturally "walk their talk."

In addition, those who open to this awareness have more resources at their disposal. Intuitive information increases and becomes readily available. Choices, perhaps hidden to others, become clear and available. This is especially important for leaders who need vision and clarity to help lead the way for others. Finally, the level of stress can decrease dramatically, providing peace and calm within as reward for committing to the inner journey.

Although the focus on external leadership skills remains a high priority today, perhaps it is time for corporations to include the inner exploration of self in their requirements for leadership. Integrity — and embracing the inner journey to obtain it — is clearly an important requirement for any leader dealing with the challenges the future promises to hold.

Chapter Five
Trust: The Foundation

Like commitment, we know trust when we have it—and it is painfully obvious when it is missing. Most would agree trust is crucial for success in any endeavor, especially in business transactions.

The literature on leadership abounds with references to trust. Current books speak to the importance of trust as a leadership trait. Often, authors write complete chapters emphasizing why leaders should create an open, trusting environment. They refer to the need for leaders to *earn* the trust of their employees and *build* trust in their organizations.

In my career, I have worked hard to earn the trust of those I managed—although I have not always achieved it. I have encouraged peers and superiors to build trust in their organizations, especially when I have been involved in leading change management or implementing quality projects.

However, as I have learned to identify and clear my own emotional blockages, I now realize that today's accepted definition of trust is limited. As my awareness has grown over the years, my own definition of trust has changed dramatically.

Expanding the Definition

When one's awareness expands, a higher form of trust naturally emerges. This higher form is unconditional and not based on experience. It comes from a deep knowing that "all is as it should be."

Unlike intention or commitment, which are tied to energies sent out into the world by an individual's thoughts, this higher state of trust is created when personal energy flows without restriction

When we meet people who exhibit this state of trust, we describe them as open, centered, understanding, and well grounded. We observe that they listen better than others. We feel comfortable talking to them and we often seek them out, especially if we want counseling or insight.

This differs from defining trust based on past experiences. That's when we draw conclusions about whom we are willing to trust from prior behavior or from our experiences with that person in a particular situation. We begin by giving the person or situation "the benefit of the doubt." But repeated experiences over time influence whether we continue to trust.

Trust and Confidence Differ

Another way we traditionally identify trust is to define it based solely on confidence. When people feel confident in a particular area, they exhibit a state that appears much like trust. In fact, we use the concept of confidence to describe this, as in "I am confident you can accomplish this task." However, an individual tuned in to subtle energies can detect the difference between feeling confident and trusting that something will occur.

Confidence comes from a place of ego; the ego *knows* through its experience what outcome will likely occur. Trust, in its purest form, comes from a different kind of "knowing" — a heartfelt belief that the outcome will align with this universal principle, *"all will be as it should be."*

In a business context, we often see the term "trust" used as a requirement of leadership. For instance, leaders must *build trust* in their organization. This phrase implies repeated acts of integrity with no room for error. It's meaning, therefore, is fragile because one incident perceived as a breach of this trust can destroy all previous efforts to build trust. Once broken, trust based on experience is almost impossible to regain.

Trust based on the ego's experience can be compared with conditional love. That's when people *give* love only when they feel assured they'd *receive* it, too. Of course, this is a "Catch 22" because this approach to trust may prevent a person from ever receiving love at all. In contrast, unconditional love is love given freely, without strings attached. This is the only true definition of love — for conditional love is not love at all. It is manipulation.

Trust is Unconditional

Like love, *unconditional* trust is the only true definition of the word. Trust based on experience has little meaning.

There is little doubt that trust — or, more appropriately, lack of trust — is a major issue in today's organizations. The success of concepts like employee empowerment programs and high performance teams is based on the premise of trust. Therefore, those who lead and run the organization must be open and trusting — not just in the ego sense but open and trusting from the heart center.

Yet the type of trust based on experience is what business leaders work so hard to obtain. In times of constant change when workers feel little stability and lose faith in their leaders, is it surprising they see trust as a hopeless goal to achieve?

So if trust is rare, how can one experience it in this higher form? More importantly, how can one *sustain* the state of unconditional trust in the hectic, inconsistent environment many organizations dwell in today?

Underlying Principles

To answer these questions, it is important to understand the underlying principles of trust. Trust requires people to focus on their inner work, clearing their own emotional blockages and releasing limiting patterns first. Once that's accomplished, they can create the space for others to do the same.

Trust is not energy; it is actually a state of being. It happens naturally when the energy of an individual is truly open and flowing. Yet it feels like a powerful force when encountered. Although this state may seem rare, each person who clears his or her energy acts as the catalyst providing the spark to generate a much-needed shift. As their presence creates trust throughout an organization, productivity and harmony increases.

Realize that trust can only be attained on an individual level. It requires being *free* of guilt or judgment of one's own actions. Truly trusting one's self precedes being able to trust others. However, as more and more people attain this state within a collective group, working together becomes an extraordinary experience, one worth getting up and going to work for!

Blocked Energy Breaks the Flow

Based on how energy flows, when one individual who is open and trusting encounters another who is blocked, the circuit of collective energy between them breaks. This, in effect, amplifies the blockage or "stuck" feeling for the person who is emotionally blocked.

It would seem logical to assume that an "open" person can successfully create a space for the "stuck" individual to safely uncover and deal with emotional blocks. Although this is true, there are times when the opposite happens. The "open" individual can unknowingly amplify the resistance, causing sparks to fly for the "stuck" individual who likely feels backed into a corner. In these situations, anger and defensiveness can erupt because he or she feels incredibly vulnerable.

Because of past conditioning, many subordinates have preconceived ideas of how a leader should "show up." Many individuals have a difficult time feeling safe in the presence of an authority figure, no matter how open the manager or supervisor may be.

To get around this barrier, the wise manager will turn to qualified resources in neutral positions, such as consultants from outside the organization. The goal is to provide a safe space for people to uncover and possibly clear the patterns that limit their performances. Professional facilitators who are centered and aware will be in high demand in those organizations willing to provide support to their work force.

Forced to Change

As individual trust grows, so does the trust within a group. Consequently, those with major energy blockages that impact group effectiveness are sometimes forced out. That is, they are forced to either face the limiting patterns affecting the group and clear them, or leave the group or organization altogether.

This happened after I facilitated a team-building process among a small management team in a computer services firm. Over the course of a year, team members repeatedly experienced serious breaches of trust. Communications among them broke down as a result. Ultimately, the business suffered. Sales and morale decreased, along with employee satisfaction and service to their customers.

Working with the concepts of energy, I helped each individual in the team uncover the limiting patterns that affected their overall effectiveness. Specifically, two key players were in a "dance of blockages" in which one person triggered a significant blockage in the other person, and vice versa. Trust had clearly broken down between these two. Other management team members found themselves having to take sides just to survive in the organization. Each of them described how draining it felt to even *be* in the office with this dance going on.

Once I understood the collective energy of this group, I knew if these two key managers could clear the limiting decisions they made about each other, the whole group would shift accordingly. So I focused my efforts on them.

With coaching, one manager got to a point of realizing the judgments he had made led him to a pattern of not trusting his colleague. That's when he clearly began to understand his role in creating the breakdown of trust and its overall impact on the rest of the group. So I supported him in approaching the other manager and explaining his revelations. He apologized for his actions and thus released his limiting decision from the past. Because of this release, he was able to return to the group with renewed focus and energy.

The other key manager only partially accepted her colleague's apology. Being unable to accept her role in creating past patterns, she remained blocked and continued the old behaviors of bitterness and blame. As the other team members responded to the new open energy created by the first manager and began to work together as a team, she became more isolated. The tactics she once used to gather team members to her side no longer worked; the rest of the team clearly wanted to get on with business in a positive way. Not knowing how to interact within a group that had put aside blame, her only option was leaving the organization.

So just a few weeks after the first manager had cleared his judgments, the second manager gave notice. She left still blaming and refusing to shift this pattern that could have opened her to trust. Not surprisingly, I learned that she re-created a similar situation in her new place of employment.

Discernment vs. Trust

As one's awareness of subtle energies increases, discernment replaces the old definition of trust based on past experiences. Discernment is the ability to understand a situation from several perspectives, and then make choices based on that understanding.

Using the power of discernment allows us to make appropriate decisions based on both direct experiences and intuitive information combined. In the new definition of trust, repeated experiences are not taken literally. Rather, they supply data to help make informed decisions.

For example, suppose that through your interaction with a colleague, you see that person is blocked in a particular area. It's important to realize the futility of expecting him or her to shift behavior in the identified area. Instead, you can be supportive in helping the individual uncover the unconscious pattern if your colleague is open to it. But expecting a different outcome without the individual identifying the source of limitations is unreasonable. Knowing this can free up enormous energy that's been wasted on hoping something will change.

Another distinction is this: when you use discernment (rather than trust based on repeated experience), you remain open to the possibility that the person or situation can shift. This creates an open space for change.

In the old definition of trust, one person automatically responds in a predictable way because of past experiences. The possibility for different outcomes arises only if the person with unconscious patterns "wakes up" and does something to rebuild the lost trust. Using discernment, the aware individual stays open to the possibility (no matter how remote it may seem) that the person could change, but wisely makes decisions that do not depend on a change to happen.

DEFINITION OF DISCERNMENT

Discernment is the ability to understand a situation from several perspectives, and then make choices based on that understanding.

Expectations Raise the Bar

Holding another person to expectations set by you can create complete havoc from an energy perspective. Because of this it is important to look at how expectations play into trust issues. In fact, expectations often *create* doubt about trust if one person does not live up to the other's expectations.

Expectations are decisions made that set a particular standard. It is one thing to set an expectation for yourself; it is far different to hold an expectation for another because that person's standard of behavior is totally out of your control. This is the perfect formula for disappointment and, in the old definition, leads to a breech of trust.

In my early career, I often held expectations about how a colleague should "show up" in the workplace. Specifically, I applied my standards to all of the bosses I had. In my eyes, I expected the person I worked for to be a true leader—someone who could guide our group through thick and thin. I also expected my boss to be open to listening, to be decisive, to resolve conflicts well.

One particular executive I worked for could never fill this tall order. As I worked with him, I realized the terror he felt when he needed to resolve conflicts. The result was a continuous undercurrent of unresolved issues in his department because he wasn't making important decisions. Situations would fester until something would finally give way and someone would blow up over specific issues.

Working in this department drained my energy tremendously. It was extremely difficult to get anything done that required agreement across functional boundaries, especially if it involved my boss. I lost respect for him, knowing he could not make the hard decisions.

Because he could not meet my expectations, I also lost all trust in his ability to lead the organization. I waited for some miracle from outside to change the situation. This in turn caused me to stall on major implementations, make excuses to my group about why we couldn't move forward, and remain in a blame orientation. Looking back, I realize I spent enormous amounts of personal energy wishing, hoping, and wanting my boss to change. I eventually left the organization in frustration.

Years later, I ran into a similar situation—a boss who struggled with making hard decisions and avoided conflict. However, I was able to look at the situation with an entirely different view. This time, I could identify the unconscious patterns my boss carried within himself. I held no judgment or expectation that he resolve conflicts. Instead, I asked him questions that helped him sort out the situation. I offered ideas that I could implement to resolve conflicts when they arose.

Certainly many times this leader's fear of resolving conflicts and making decisions had a negative impact. He did cause things to get blocked in the organization. But I did not try to change him, nor did I expect him to "show up" any way other than the way he did. This proved to be incredibly freeing for me.

I always held the possibility he might clear the blocks, yet I never *expected* it. Knowing this, I never wasted my time on how things *should be* in that organization. Instead, I spent my energy creating a foundation in the areas I could influence. When I realized I had done all I could within the limitations of his leadership, I began to look for my next position. Interestingly enough, he left the organization just as I was beginning my exploration. This opened whole new possibilities for me. I ended up staying awhile and reached another level that would have been impossible if he had remained in the organization.

DEFINITION OF EXPECTATIONS

Expectations are decisions made that set a particular standard for yourself or others.

Acknowledge the Situation

It is important to identify and acknowledge when you are working directly with someone who is blocked in ways that are key to your work. This lets you assess what is possible and what is not. In addition, it is important to identify for yourself what expectations you hold for this individual.

When you take time to determine you are working with an individual whose energy is blocked (and accept that fact), you can bring forth new possibilities. At the least, doing this lets you choose to put your precious energy in another arena that is more fulfilling.

This begs the question, "What if the blocked person is on the critical path of a task I want to accomplish?" This happens often. Yet the answer remains the same: Use discernment to identify and accept the situation as vital information, then make choices. Next ask, "What needs to happen so I can accomplish the task at hand?" The key to getting results is to stop judging or holding certain expectations, so accept that the person with the limiting patterns is doing the best he or she can. Then let new possibilities arise...including the possibility that person will also grow from the experience.

Trust Attained from Within

Since trust is not energy, it cannot be given or taken away. One cannot *demand* trust of another person. Yet so many people use the phrase "I need your trust" like it is something one gives out on demand. The phrase "you have to earn my trust" is equally invalid, for the centered person trusts freely and does not put conditions on the level of trust given. And since trust in its highest form is a state of being in which energy flows, *the only place to attain it is from oneself.*

However, since trust is a state of being, individuals can readily model it. A leader who is centered and aligned with universal principle creates an environment that is conducive for others to adopt the same state. When the leader "walks the talk," it helps others reach the same state of being.

Even those unwilling to accept the possibility of unconditional trust will experience an open leader or colleague as a person of integrity. They are likely to trust those who display unconditional trust, even if mistakes are made, for mistakes will be recognized as just that—mistakes rather than intentional acts. Conversely, when leaders or colleagues cannot demonstrate unconditional trust, others may assume mistakes are intentional. An environment filled with suspicion often results.

To the leaders who understand and model trust in its truest sense, it makes no difference what others' believe. A deep inner certainty is an additional benefit of attaining a high form of trust within one's self. Recognizing the power of discernment and understanding the proper placement of expectations, they create an environment that is open and fair—certainly a place where people want to work.

Chapter Six
Intuition: The Inner Guide

Have you ever had a hunch that suddenly came true? Acting on a "gut" feeling about something probably happens far more often than is acknowledged in the workplace.

Leaders from all ages have used this sixth-sense to make decisions when the variables were too many or the time too short to analyze the facts. Yet this skill is still vastly ignored when it comes to management or leadership development. Based on a Newtonian view, only input from our five senses is deemed valid when making decisions in our organizations.

At best, we substantiate hunches and "gut" feelings with reams of information gathered and processed by staff people who support the leader. At worst, we ignore intuitive insights altogether. Why? Because the information seems to come from nowhere—at least not from any place the other five senses can identify. Also, the information from our "gut" feelings seems to be random and unpredictable. Yet intuition can be developed like any other skill. When people quiet their minds and get centered, their natural intuitive abilities become much more accessible and predictable.

The most important ingredient to opening the sixth-sense is simply the *intention* to do so. Like learning any other skill, people first need to *want* to learn this skill, and then they must *believe* they can learn it.

In fact, intuition can be regarded as an advanced listening skill because it is the ability to receive messages from a deep place within. That place taps into the vast energetic field of information that bombards human beings moment to moment. Like radio or television signals that require the right equipment to tune in to the station, intuition is the ability to "tune in" to appropriate information, as well.

Invoking and Cultivating Intuition

There are four simple steps to begin to open and use your intuitive ability: (1) embrace the fact that intuition is a natural ability, (2) use intention or a question to access specific information, (3) quiet your mind, and (4) trust the message received.

Most important is to act on the information you receive. As you become more confident, you will use this information like any other vital information you receive through logic or your other senses. And like any other skill, you need to use intuition continually so you can build the competence you need to benefit from it. Let's look at what you need for each step.

The first step may sound easy enough, yet it is often the biggest obstacle encountered when people begin to intentionally access their intuition. In a business setting, the added pressure and conditioning of using the rational mind creates even more obstacles. So *believe* it is possible. Better yet, believe it is a latent talent you have always had.

When I work with people who are starting to be conscious about their intuition, I begin by asking questions that unearth their beliefs about their sixth-sense.

Most people are aware of their hunches; they just *knew* something was going to happen. Yet, the idea of tapping into their hunches on a regular basis doesn't always occur to them. So when I ask, "What do you believe about intuition in general?" most people accept that the ability to be intuitive does exist. Yet, when I ask what beliefs they hold about their *own* intuitive ability, the answers vary. They range from: "everyone has the ability to be intuitive" to "it is something supernatural that should not be tampered with." Sadly, many fail to claim this skill for themselves. Occasionally, I find some who just don't want to know. Why? Because if they accepted the premise, then they'd have to be responsible for the information received.

So taking a look at your own beliefs will help you see if anything stands in the way of cultivating this capability. If you identify a belief that may inhibit your intuition, take time to explore the decision that formed the belief. Once identified, look at what new decision might better support developing your intuition. Continue to look at this as you progress through the process.

FOUR STEPS TO INVOKING INTUITION

1. **Embrace your intuition as a natural ability.**

2. **Use an intention or a question to access specific information.**

3. **Quiet your mind.**

4. **Trust the message.**

Making "Gut" Decisions

In the Introduction, I described my fateful experience when I told my boss I was going to leave my position to follow my heart. After I had admitted to a life outside of work that included giving intuitive readings, Mike asked if I thought *he* was intuitive.

I had no doubt that Mike was intuitive; in fact, I saw him use it on a day-to-day basis. He often made decisions with his "gut," as he would say. When he received information from his staff that seemed to contradict his intuition or didn't lead to a decisive conclusion, Mike would take a deep breath and contemplate for a moment. Then he would announce his decision.

Other times, when the decision needed was complex or he didn't want to trust his "gut," he would ask staff members (including me) to research the issue. When this occurred, we knew he was looking for proof to confirm what his keen sixth-sense had already told him. Much research within the halls of organizations is just that—confirmation of a leader's inner knowing.

Finding Your Natural Ability

To find out how natural this ability is, think of a time when you had a hunch about something and it turned out to be "right on." Take a moment to relive the experience. Close your eyes and bring it fully into your conscious awareness. Now ask yourself, how did you receive this hunch? Notice any feelings in your body that accompanied the knowing message. Did you *see* the message? Did a voice say it to you? Did you have a sudden thought that seemed to come from nowhere?

You can repeat this exercise with other insights you have had. You should begin to see a pattern emerge that shows how you "tune in" to intuitive information. I always get a tingling feeling; then I know. However, the response is unique to each person; there is no right or wrong way to tune in.

Once you identify how you receive this information, it's easy to invoke it whenever you require additional information. Step two uses intention to guide, focus, and access information from your intuitive channel. The key is to clarify what you intend to access. This can be accomplished by forming a simple question.

Notice I said, "simple question." When starting out, simple is better. As you gain more confidence, you can go for more complex questions. However, after doing this for many years, I still like to break down a broad inquiry into simple components. For instance, you may find yourself stressed due to a difficult workload. Say that even after dealing with the priorities, you still can't accomplish what is needed. In this case, you could ask, "What must I do at this time?" This will likely elicit a different answer than your analytical mind brought forth.

The third step is to quiet your mind, focusing only on the intention or question you formed in step two. A quiet mind provides the gateway to the intuitive part of the brain. Emptying the mind of extraneous thoughts running rampant in the analytical side of the brain allows space for the intuitive side to come through more clearly.

Once your mind is quiet and you are holding the question, just listen. Pay particular attention to the avenue by which you normally receive your intuitive information. Remember to listen deeply and accept the first message that comes forth. The first piece of information usually comes from intuition; what often follows is the analytical mind analyzing the intuitive information.

It is not unusual for the analytical mind to grab onto the information and run with it. Once this occurs, stop, re-center yourself, quiet your mind, and start over. Train yourself to be sure you are receiving the complete intuitive message before logic takes over. *This takes practice.* Don't be hard on yourself if you find it difficult to stay in the intuitive frame of mind. The more you notice and stop to re-center, the sooner you will see the subtle distinctions between the analytical and the intuitive.

I often access my intuitive ability to move "out of the trees" so I can see the whole "forest." I use questions like: "How can I look at this matter differently? What am I missing? What is the most important thing I must know about a given matter? What is going on behind the scenes?" Again, asking these questions from a quiet mind yields a deeper, more intuitive answer than asking these questions when the mind is rapidly moving from point to point.

The fourth step is about trusting the message that comes through. Often, it is not what you expected. Yet intuitive messages are actually the easiest ones to trust because you know your rational mind didn't come up with them. If the message is exactly what you expected, take another moment to clear your mind and center your body. Check in one more time, just to make sure. Ask the question from a slightly different angle. As you practice more, you will be able to discern even the slightest differences between information that comes from your rational mind versus from an intuitive place.

To build muscle in this area, keep an intuition journal. Take time at the end of the day (or whenever it works for you) to note recent experiences when you received intuitive information.

The more incidents you can document, the more insight you will have on how you naturally access and work with your intuition. Make a note of the insights, when and how you received them. Then comment on what actually happened. When you begin to ask specific questions, document the answers to your inquiries in your journal, then compare that information to what actually happened. Use this four-step process to build your confidence in your intuitive ability.

IDENTIFY HOW YOU NATURALLY ACCESS INTUITION

1. Think of a time when you had a hunch or intuition in advance of some event.

   a. Go deep into the experience, remembering what you saw, heard, and felt.

   b. Recall how you received the intuitive message — was it a voice, a thought, a feeling, etc.

   c. Repeat the experience with other examples until you identity a pattern that tells you how you typically receive intuitive information.

2. Use intention, forming a simple question or objective to access specific intuitive information.

3. Quiet your mind, focusing only on your question.

4. Trust the first message that comes through. Keep good notes to continue to build your trust in your intuitive information.

5. Act on the information.

Finally, act on the information you received. As your confidence grows, you will be more likely to use the information as part of your natural decision process. When this begins to happen, you will have made major progress in integrating your intuitive ability into your daily life — including work.

Balancing Intuition and Reason

Intuitive information can confirm what you see in the world of facts and numbers. Yet, at times, it can seem to make no sense at all.

An intuitive answer to a simple question may defy current trends. It may seem totally contrary to the direction you are heading. It could bring forth something so controversial that you question what to do with this information. Certainly if you mention something like this, others will think you are crazy — how could you ever tell your colleagues how you arrived at this conclusion or direction?

Interestingly enough, this process has given birth to some of the most profound breakthroughs. Great scientists and thinkers throughout history have brought new insights into the world through the intuitive process. Einstein, for example, would have dreams or flashes of understanding that would take years to prove from the standpoint of the rational mind.

We can use the intuitive process as a way to breakthrough a complex situation or it can invoke our creative abilities. Creativity is a great example of the play between our intuitive and rational minds. Through intuition, we often seed creative new ideas. Then, through our rational minds, we find ways to apply them in our day-to-day world.

When to Use Intuition

We live in a time when an innovation deficit plagues large organizations. Bureaucracy is often cited for the lack of creativity. However, having an extreme focus on the analytical mind doesn't allow us to tap into the intuitive side on a regular basis. Accessing the intuitive can bring individuals and groups to a place of new ideas and possibilities.

When I was a software developer, I took great pride in my analytical ability to resolve issues — both technical ones and those having to do with my project team. I used logic as my guide, pouring over options and various strategies. Looking back, no doubt I had moments when an idea or thought did come from somewhere other than my rational mind. But these insights happened unconsciously. At that time, it never occurred to me that intuition could become a conscious part of the equation.

Later, as I began to intentionally develop my intuitive ability in my spare time, it still did not occur to me to use it at work. This may seem strange, yet I share this because I know many feel they lack permission to bring this ability to work. The truth is, as I embraced my intuition and gave myself permission to tap into it in my day-to-day business life, I simplified my work life. Now, whether I am perplexed about an issue or feel something is amiss and I want to get a handle on its cause, I turn to intuition. Doing this has brought an ease and flow into my routine that was absent in my early career.

I often use intuition to help determine my priorities, especially when the list of top priorities exceeds the time available. I simply quiet my mind and ask, "What is the most important thing for me to accomplish at this time?"

It is often amazing the added insights I receive by simply asking, "What task should I focus on *now?*" Many times, the answer was not the task I would have chosen. Yet, trusting the answer I get and moving forward with the task — time and time again — has proven to be wise.

For instance, many times I have received an intuitive message to call someone on my contact list right away. That specific call wasn't a priority for that day. Yet, when I connected with the person, I learned he or she would not have been available when I had originally planned to call.

In one particular situation, I was scanning my call list and received an urgent intuitive message to call someone I didn't need to contact for a week. Acting on this information, I called and soon learned she was going to be out of the country for a long time, starting the week I had originally planned to call. Waiting to call her would have created delays for many people, including me.

Imagine this scenario occurring several times over. You can begin to see how tapping into this resource regularly can create ease and flow in a typical business day.

Using Intuition at Work

Use your intuitive ability when something just doesn't feel right. For instance, you might have a project that shows signs of delay—like missed deadlines or feedback that sounds like excuses. Typically, when faced with this, you start to identify the source of the issue so you can take corrective action.

Instead, take a moment to go within. Asking your intuition a few important questions can shorten this analysis process and help you zero in on where to go first. In such a situation, I begin by asking, "What is the source of the issue?" At times, the answer may confirm what I am already observing. But more often then not, another piece of information will come forth that I hadn't considered.

Again, this approach does not *replace* the planning or diagnostic tools you use. In fact, you can better use intuition to focus on where to use these tools. I still do planning as I always have. But I use intuitive questions to augment my status process along the way. To honor those working with me, I use this information to form questions for my team. These questions get at the concerns I have uncovered and will help head off minor issues before they become major ones.

Also, I use my intuition to understand what is happening with a remote situation, such as with a customer. One time when I was working with a customer contact to set up a series of trainings, everything was going along smoothly until suddenly I couldn't reach her. I knew something had happened, but I wasn't sure what.

I accessed my intuition and asked, "What is happening at this client location?" I got a strong sense of turmoil and confusion. Based on this information, I had a feeling some major reorganization must have been announced. I continued the process by asking, "Will this delay the training project?" I got a definite "yes." So I immediately reduced my estimates by taking the projected revenue numbers from this customer out of my plan.

Several days later, I finally received an apologetic call from my contact. She said a major reorganization had just been announced; she was calling to postpone the project for six months.

Complex Inquiries: Continuing the Dialog

Complex decisions offer a great opportunity to tap into your intuition. If a situation offers a range of options—all of which seem feasible in one way or another—use intuition to pick the best one for the situation. Form your questions specifically, asking, "What is the highest or best option for this situation?" Once you have your answer, you can always ask more questions to determine *why* this is the best option.

Remember, *you can always go back and ask more questions*. It's easy to forget this in the excitement of receiving the first answer.

After one program I gave on integrating intuition in the work environment, a woman asked me, "What do you do when you know someone is blocked and you see possible ways to help the person see it, but you don't know how to approach this person?"

I said to go back inside and ask: "What do I do with this information? What is my role in supporting this individual?" The answer may not include pointing this out to the person involved. You have likely received the information so you can be ready to provide support, if and when the person triggers an opening.

This was a major learning for me. I used to feel responsible when I received a message on behalf of another person. In the workplace, going up to someone and saying you received an intuitive message about him or her can evoke a negative reaction. However, when I ask, "What is the purpose of me receiving this information and what do I do with it?" then I can take appropriate action on it.

Is This Mine to Do?

In fact, I have reduced enormous amounts of stress in my work by *always* stopping before I take corrective action and asking, "Is this mine to do?" If the answer comes back "yes," then I ask, "What is my role in this?'

In my early management days, I would respond to every inquiry, conflict, issue, or crisis that came my way. After all, I was the manager! Now I realize that is not necessarily the best approach. Many times when I am approached with an issue, I quickly go within to access the best response or action for this individual. I often receive a question back that will help the person discover the answer for him or herself.

Sometimes I receive information that helps me realize there is something major for this individual to learn by working through it. That's when I turn the question right back and ask, "What do you think you should do?" In other cases, I may simply state the truth and say, "I believe there is something for you to learn and I trust whatever decisions you make concerning this situation."

Always, I balance this intuitive answer with the urgency of the situation. There are definitely times when immediate intervention is necessary, either through intuitive inquiry or rationally knowing that deadlines or other pressures need to be considered. However, these emergencies happen less frequently than we think. The more times we follow our intuition and allow others to discover and learn, the fewer times we will have to intervene later.

When to Do Nothing

Finally, intuition can be used to determine when to do *nothing*. This may seem like a radical concept, but again, it has been one of the most stress-relieving tools I have discovered in my later years as a leader.

First of all, just *realizing* that doing nothing was an option took a while to comprehend. The more I invoked intuition for complex decisions, the more I began to get "nothing for you to do on this" or "wait, this is not the right time to act" as a response. At first, I didn't trust this as a valid answer. But as I worked with it more, I realized the great wisdom of this decision.

In times before, I would struggle against the odds or push against things out of my control. Now, I have the understanding to wait and, if necessary, direct my available energy (and the energy of those who report to me) to areas that later prove to be the most productive.

Building Intuitive Muscle

This chapter has offered a basic introduction to tapping into your intuitive ability. There are many good books about intuition that can help "build muscle" and deepen your personal use of this ability. One of my favorites is *The Intuitive Way: A Guide to Living From Inner Wisdom* by Penney Peirce, Beyond Words Publishing, Inc. This book provides the guidance and exercises to open to your intuitive abilities through the inner journey

The best part of working with your intuition is that nobody needs to know! So have fun and explore new possibilities with it. Ask about areas that truly are not visible to you. Take good notes on what is revealed through your inner knowing. Then watch what plays out. Comparing notes, you may be surprised at just how easy it is to manage, incorporating your intuitive ability into most everything you do.

Chapter Seven
Communication: The Link

Everywhere we look, communication is an issue. Whether it is connecting on the World Wide Web or the age-old method of speaking and listening, communication—and the need to improve communication—is a hot topic.

In the workplace, everyone wants more of it—communication. If you wander in the halls or walk the assembly lines of most companies, workers will tell you they want more communication from management. Managers want better communication with their employees, peers, executives, and with other areas of the company. And so it goes, everyone longing for more clear and open communication.

Actually, the key words are "clear" and "open," not "more." People are bombarded by communication from every direction. Computers produce more information than our predecessors ever had to deal with. Media of all types barrage us with instant news updates and issues of the day—constantly. And, of course, on the Internet we can tap into information on any topic imaginable.

Forms of communication have increased dramatically, with the proliferation of computer networks and advancement of voice-data technology. The Internet, electronic mail, voice messaging, video conferencing (just to name a few) allow us to communicate messages throughout our companies at lightning speeds regardless of distance.

Despite this information frenzy, people crave *clear* and *open* communication. In fact, even with this information overload, many remain in the dark about what's going on in their work environment. Ironically, more technology has allowed us to increase the amount of information that is communicated. Yet it has also decreased the amount of interaction we experience with fellow human beings. The question is this, "How can we improve simple interactions with our colleagues and truly communicate?"

Communication: What Is It?

Let's look at how communication works in terms of subtle energy. Understanding it will help bring more clarity and authenticity to this element that everyone uses every day.

If we ask people to define what excellent or even good communication looks like (and how they know when it has occurred), we get varied answers. Those versed in communication theory will explain it takes at least two entities: the sender of a message and its receiver. That is, no matter how clear the sender's message might be, it will *only* get through if the receiver is open to listening.

Even with a well-thought-out message, receivers can alter it as it moves through their maze of beliefs. Beliefs serve as filters to all information each of us receives. And to complicate matters, clear messages are in short supply—for they require the senders to *know* what points they want to get across.

Materials on improving communications tend to focus on data that pertains to the five senses—primarily speaking and listening, with some visual queues to identify incongruence in what was said.

Yet communication based on sensory input and output merely *confirms* the actual communication that is taking place on the subtle energy level. As described in the chapter on Energy, thoughts are energy. Thoughts also precede the spoken word. Energy thought forms are released to the world prior to the spoken word or without any word spoken at all. Therefore, a thought is available to be received before any physical communication takes place.

Those who believe in accepting insight from their intuition acknowledge the information the moment a thought form is created. Shifting our beliefs *to accepting that thoughts can be received before the senses confirm them* totally changes the way we look at communication. If thought forms precede physical communication, then focusing our thoughts clearly can dramatically influence communication overall.

Be Centered in the Moment

Here's the key. To focus our thoughts clearly, we need to be centered in the moment.

Consider a world in which all individuals live fully centered in the present moment—both those conveying a message and those in a receptive state to receive the message. With this scenario, communication problems as they exist today would vanish.

Communication training rarely addresses areas such as *quieting the mind* or *being centered*. The techniques most often taught do not get at the root of the problems with real communication and are therefore only marginally successful. Once again, we find that providing support at the level of a disciplined mind and heart treads into an area few business professionals have explored.

Since our thoughts and intentions play such a key role in the results of communication, looking at it from the perspective of inner awareness can lead to some dramatic improvements. A skilled communicator who discovers internal blocks and takes time to clear them will unleash new levels of authenticity. His or her audience will know the difference. The ability to inspire and motivate others comes from this deep knowing of self. This, in turn, opens us to a greater understanding of others.

Teaching communication from the perspective of energy gets at the core issues of creating clear, open, and congruent communication. *Improving* it at this level can make a positive impact when dealing with conflict, setting intention, or doing an intervention involving group dynamics.

The point is this: The clarity and quality of our communication—either written or spoken—is greatly affected by the state of our energy field.

Let's take a deeper look at both sides of communication—sending and receiving—beginning with the formation and delivery of a message.

Delivering a Message

Simple communication refers to the communication that takes place between two people. (Later, we will address the issues in communicating messages online, with a group, or collectively.)

As mentioned above, our thoughts precede our spoken words. Therefore, what goes on in our thoughts drives how we will deliver a particular message. No matter how the sender tries to cover up those thoughts—that is, speaking a message different than the actual thoughts—the *true* information is always available to the person receiving the message.

This is the essence of the phrase "walking the talk," in which thoughts, words, and actions completely align. Often, if our words have been carefully altered to supposedly conceal the actual thoughts, our actions give them away, revealing what is really going on. This can be subtle—such as in body language or tone of voice—or it can be more obvious as saying one thing and doing another.

Misaligned behavior happens a hundred times a day. Employees, peers and superiors—not to mention friends and loved ones—all do it. Incongruent messages from political figures especially stand out. But how often do we look at our own communication? And what do others understand when we communicate with them?

Learning to become conscious of our thoughts before we speak leads to creating clear, open, congruent communication at work. This sounds simple, but it feels difficult at first because we normally communicate on an unconscious level. We rarely think twice about how we interact with others, yet any blocks or conflicts within our energy fields will affect the messages we send.

Creating Clear Messages

A typical manager spends a great deal of time communicating requests for information and tasks needing to be accomplished, as well as giving feedback to others. Add to that the usual conversations on the status of projects and actions taken. All of these conversations create an opportunity for clear, open communication and provide a view of how well the managers "walk their talk."

Preparing for an important communication—such as giving feedback to an employee or making a request to a boss—involves several steps. This may seem like a lot to think about but the steps become easier with increased practice and awareness. Over time, the following questions can become second nature—simple questions you run on any time you need to convey information.

First, quiet your mind and center your body using the techniques described in the Integrity chapter. Do this when you prepare the message and again when you are about to deliver it. This practice provides focus and helps you gain rapport with the person you want to communicate *to*.

Next, ask yourself, "What do I want as a result of this communication?" Think about this from the point of your needs and the needs of the person you are communicating *to*. Are you conveying status and wanting the person to be informed? Do you need this person to agree to take a specific action? Are you providing feedback, expecting something to change in this person's behavior?

Then, play the communication in your mind and observe the probable reaction of the person you will be communicating to. Determine the likely response of the recipient. If you get the outcome you desire, your communication is complete. However, if you notice some resistance or the message does not get through, look deeper to consider the possible cause.

Be sure to consider what blocks might be operating for others. Are they in fear about something related to this communication? If you are asking them to take on a project, are they overloaded with other priorities? Whatever the situation, take a moment to assess this and determine how you might alter your message to obtain a better outcome.

Perhaps you need to convey another message before you deliver the actual piece of communication. This might simply acknowledge the reality the person currently faces. It might openly state your intention before making your request or delivering your message. Whatever it is, it will lead to a deeper rapport with this individual so your message will more likely get through.

Now when you *deliver* the message(s), quiet your mind and center your body again. Focusing on your breath will make this happen in a short time. You can actually do this in the time it takes to dial the person's phone number or walk to the person's office.

Preparing the content of your message will vastly increase the number of effective communications for you. Yet, if you do receive resistance while delivering the message or something arises you did not foresee, ask questions to identify what is coming up. Then listen carefully to the answers. If you request something and the person hesitates or refuses the action, ask, "What stops you from taking this on?" If the person becomes angry or agitated, ask, "What is this bringing up for you?"

Continue to probe to get to the receiver's underlying issue. Remember, sometimes communications can inadvertently trigger blocks that are hidden. So keep your center and remember *this unconscious pattern belongs to the other person* — not you! The more centered you remain (including staying detached from the outcome), the more resources you will have to steer through the issue(s).

STEPS TO PREPARE A CLEAR MESSAGE

1. Quiet your mind and center your body.

2. Ask, "What outcome do I want to create with this communication?"

   a. "What outcome do I want to create for the other person?"

   b. "What outcome do I need?"

3. Play the communication over in your mind, observing the probable reaction.

4. Revise the message based on what you learn from Step 3.

Judgments Affect Communication

Any limiting decision or judgment that may be in your way concerning the receiver can affect your communication. In fact, any judgment you hold concerning the individual can totally change the message another person receives. So, take a moment to consider what limiting decisions you may hold that the recipient may experience. Understanding this may cause you to alter your message as well.

Many examples in this book illustrate how judgments can impact the overall effectiveness of one's interaction with another. Remember the example of the woman colleague who remained in my sphere of influence until I recognized my own issues of control? This shows how judgments can influence one's communication. My communication with her always seemed forced or restricted, making it difficult to tell the truth or express what I needed from her to accomplish the project at hand.

In the beginning, I believed *she* caused these limitations. In part that was true, for she did have her own issues of control that blocked her energy. However, as I was able to identify and shift judgments I held about her, my own communication improved. I found ways to speak to her about my requirements without playing into her issues of control.

In my early communications with this colleague, I felt furious that I had to deal with her. She annoyed me. I believed my annoyance was due to her need to control and her lack of follow-through. Needless to say, our communication was strained. I tried different strategies to out control her — none of which worked.

Finally, I looked at what she was mirroring for me. I realized I had *my own* issues around control and lack of follow-through. It was hard to face, but once I realized it, I began to see her in a new light. Our communication improved dramatically. Once I understood her need, I made sure to follow my requests by asking questions like: "What would work for you? Is this possible? In what time frame can you get back to me on this?" I also made sure I gave her lots of opportunity to put her "two cents" in.

How Do You Know It's Improved?

One way to know if your communication has improved is by checking your level of resistance. When the resistance you once felt disappears within you, improvement has taken place. Once this happens, you may develop a rapport that never showed up before.

This was certainly true for my colleague and me. Once I became aware of my judgments, I gained a level of rapport with her I had never experienced before. Having this rapport allowed me to listen and understand her motivations and needs. This in turn helped me communicate even more effectively with her. It also lessened the impact of my playing into her issues and led to win-win scenarios. I could get what I needed without creating resistance for her.

When we shift our limiting judgments about someone, we are also able to notice more readily when communication adversely affects the other person. If we can remain open and centered, we will find it easy to ask questions that may shift the resistance for the other. This, in turn, allows us to identify more effective ways to communicate our message and create the outcome we intended in the first place.

So judgments we make about a person or situation actually prevent us from communicating in an open manner. *Just trying to be open simply doesn't work.* What *does* work is looking at our own reaction and using it to discover our own limiting patterns, then *clearing* these patterns. Using the exercises from the Energy chapter will open the door to more clear and open communications with others.

Mixed Messages

When preparing your message, take time to ask, "What is your intention in delivering this message?" This question leads to discovering two things: the subtle decisions you have made and the areas in which your thoughts and words are incongruent with each other.

Subtle (and sometimes not so subtle) communication distortions can occur when the message you try to deliver does not agree with the decisions you have made. Performance reviews in particular provide opportunities to take a look at subtle decisions or judgments.

As a former professional services director, I often supported managers preparing to engage in difficult discussions with their employees. In one instance, I was helping a manager prepare to talk with an employee whose performance was not meeting the requirements of the position. The manager had already warned him of what had to change. In the manager's eyes, he had made some effort; however, more issues had to be addressed and the employee appeared to be struggling.

At this point, the manager wanted to give the employee more feedback and deliver a more severe warning than before. He struggled with how to deliver the message so it would make a difference. As I listened to him describing the situation, I asked, "Do you believe this employee will make it?"

"No," came the simple reply.

I then went through a line of questioning to help the manager discover the decisions *he had already made*. The manager admitted he already believed the position was not ideal for this employee—it required skills and activities the employee found difficult.

Through my probing, he realized his conflict between the message he thought he *should* deliver and the truth of the decision he had already made. As a result, he changed his focus to helping the employee leave his current position. From there, new choices opened.

The conversation between the manager and employee that followed allowed the employee to admit he felt miserable in the position. Indeed, he felt relieved when his manager talked about the possibility his job was not a fit for him. In the end, the employee began a search that led him to a whole new career. And he left the company on the best of terms.

At work, we can find ourselves trying to communicate what *should* be communicated. This is true no matter if it's leaders delivering talks on company results or employees communicating the status of their projects.

Remember that we send out our thoughts before our words, so others pick up on the real message. This can lead to problems. If a leader delivers a mixed message to the masses, the subordinates can tell the leader is not "walking the talk." If a subordinate provides status only on what a superior wants to hear, that person knows something is "fishy." Both situations provide an opportunity for one party to distrust the other. Therefore, being aware of our judgments, decisions, and intentions is crucial for delivering messages that are clear and congruent.

When Blocks Get Triggered

When your communication elicits a negative emotional reaction in the other person, pay attention. This may be an opportunity to support the other individual in identifying what is being triggered. Whether you feel it is appropriate to intervene in this matter or not, a simple line of questioning will at the very least help you detect what is going on.

Start by asking: "What is coming up for you?" or "What did that trigger for you?" As always, give the person plenty of space and time to answer the question. If you sense there's more after the initial answer, ask, "What else is there?" Your role is to facilitate the discovery of the issue(s) for the person.

No matter how open and centered you are — or how well meaning your message may be — you can still trigger a reaction in another person. In most cases, it pays to discover what is going on.

For example, one situation involved a fairly senior staff member who reported to me. Every time I made a simple request of this person, I encountered incredible resistance. Sometimes he would ignore or conveniently forget what I had requested; other times I'd receive a response that sounded like an excuse. Then there were times when I received an angry retort or a defiant "no."

This occurred once when I was just beginning to learn how to use these concepts, so I was reluctant at first to ask what was being triggered for this person. Instead, I began with these questions: "What support do you need to make that happen?" and "When can you have this by?" I would go to great lengths to help the individual understand the importance of carrying this action out—why it was needed and how it would be used.

With this effort on my part, I was able to reduce the number of angry retorts, but still had only marginal results when it came to his meeting the requirements.

Finally, in a meeting planned to give him feedback, I broached the topic carefully. I asked what was triggered for him when I made requests of him. He revealed his struggles with his demanding father. Being the youngest of three, he'd developed a pattern of avoiding or procrastinating—hoping one of the older siblings would take care of it. This conversation not only helped our communication, it also helped him break a pattern that had cost him dearly for 25 years.

Receiving a Message

Listening deeply to another person is one of the greatest gifts you can give. In business, this gift is rare. Yet, just as it's important for a leader to communicate clear messages to his or her organization, it's also important to have the ability to be present and open to the communication of others—if not more so. The individual who masters this ability will earn the respect and appreciation of others in the organization—no matter what level they reside in.

Many of the same principles discussed in creating a message apply when receiving a message. The ability to listen deeply comes not from skill but from a state of being—that calm, centered mind. In this fast-paced world, is it any wonder listening is in short supply?

Quieting the mind and centering the body when *receiving* communications creates a natural state for listening deeply. As I put these concepts into practice in my business world, I'm amazed at the depth of understanding that has emerged for me. I quickly "catch" myself when someone wants to tell me something and I am not present.

This happens when I'm in the middle of a project and someone walks into my office to tell me something. I quickly realize I'm missing much of that person's message. If I really *can't* be interrupted, I ask if we could schedule a better time to talk. If I *can* be interrupted, I politely apologize and take a moment to center and focus my mind on the present moment. Then I ask the individual to start over. The person always appreciates getting my undivided attention.

Just as in delivering a message, a judgment or limiting decision can interfere with one's ability to hear the message fully. At times, a communication from someone clearly triggers a block within you—often suddenly and unexpectedly. Feeling resistance or a negative emotional reaction to a message provides an opportunity to find the source of the block or conflict within.

If you find yourself in this situation, notice your breath. Does it become shallow when something is triggered? Take a moment to breathe and re-center your body. This will not clear the block but it *will* give you some time to re-group and make a choice, rather than follow an unconscious reaction.

After leaving the situation that triggered the reaction, take a moment to return to the exercises described in the Energy chapter. That will help you identify and clear the issue that has surfaced for you.

Experience what a difference a quiet mind can make when you are listening to another. In a future conversation, take a moment to still your mind and center your body with focused breathing. Then engage in the conversation and fully listen to the other person. What do you notice? What do you hear that you might not have heard in previous conversations? How long does it take for your mind to start figuring out your response?

The longer you can stay in the centered state, the better your response will be. It only takes a moment to formulate your message back, anyway. So why take up time that can provide you with more vital information? In addition to gaining clarity and information, you will obtain a deeper level of rapport with the individual communicating to you. For that person, being *heard* is an incredible gift to receive.

Communicating with the Collective

These same principles apply when speaking to groups or a large audience. But what becomes even more important is the clarity of your intention—understanding the outcome you want. Your own congruency plays a bigger role when you're speaking in front of a large audience instead of one-on-one. In addition, it's important to tap into what is going on for your audience.

Here's the challenge you have working with collective energy: You can't please everyone because you're speaking to a collective pool of individual energies. Yet within any group—from a project team to an entire organization—the individuals have bought into several themes. That's why they are a part of this particular group. So the question becomes, "Where does the majority stand in relation to the topics you need to speak about?"

You may have to pay attention to much more than just the message when speaking to groups. I personally learned this the hard way. In my early career, I would focus on what I needed to say, strictly in terms of what message I needed to put out. My approach was quite simple—convey the facts and nothing but the facts!

As a project manager in charge of computer software development projects, this seemed to work. After all, I usually communicated messages about project direction and schedules. But as my career advanced and I became more involved with the direction of the organization, I realized I had to change my ways.

The turning point came when I became general manager of a branch of a software services firm. Within six months of being promoted, a serious situation threatened our market. Most of the consultants in our branch knew the large banking software systems and more than 60 percent of our revenue came from the computer centers of several large banks in the area. Unfortunately, a series of bank mergers wiped out our customer base within a matter of months. Three large computer centers that provided much of our business closed in our area and moved out of state. I realized we needed to shift the skill-set in the branch and broaden into other areas.

While dealing with this issue, I learned about a huge outsourcing opportunity in another city, so we proceeded to get into the bidding process to win the business. Winning this account would create another branch in a city distant from our current location, yet still in my region. In my mind (and my boss's mind as well), this opportunity could help solve the market loss we faced in our current area. It could also provide opportunities for the consultants willing to relocate.

This entire scenario created a wealth of communication challenges as I tried to keep my anxious staff members at all levels informed of the changes. I held several staff meetings to communicate what was taking place. As I had in the past, I simply communicated the situation as I saw it at each point along the path. Everyone knew the situation with the banks; after all, it was spread across the news headlines every day. We started helping the staff retrain in newer computer languages. But time wasn't on our side; many of the consultants doubted they could compete with those who already had the skills and experience.

Still, I felt excited about the new opportunity and conveyed that to the group. My staff, though, didn't share that feeling. They were in a place of great fear, believing the writing was on the wall for their jobs. My excitement about the new opportunity indicated *to them* that I was abandoning the current location.

In the end, we won the business — the largest opportunity in one city ever to be won by our company. For me, it should have been a time to celebrate, but it turned out to be bittersweet. A satisfaction survey of my staff in our home location reflected the pain and fear that had built over that whole year. They turned to upper management and asked to have me removed from my position.

Ironically, I had improved the employee satisfaction rating of that branch substantially in the prior year when I had been assistant manager. Now, only one year later, I'd lost everything I'd achieved and more.

Process for Speaking to a Group

I can look back at this situation and see several things I would have done differently — especially the messages I delivered over that year. I didn't take the time to fully tap into the energy of my staff and clearly decide the result I wanted to achieve with the messages I delivered. If I had done this, the outcome would have been radically different.

Now I follow a simpler process, similar to the steps needed to create a clear message. I hope you will use it for yourself. Here are the steps:

Start by identifying the message you want to deliver. Ask yourself: "What outcome do I want to create with this message? What will be different because of this communication? What is the ideal state I wish to achieve by communicating this information?" Pay close attention to how you want your audience to feel as a result of this message. Then focus on what you want to be different because of this communication, especially in terms of their actions.

Then determine if your message aligns with this outcome. Is there anything you would change when communicating this message, based on any new information? Take notes and continue.

Now, holding that message in your mind, tap into the energy of your audience members. Where are they in relation to this message? How will they react to it? What might it bring up for them?

Allow yourself to notice what you see, hear, and feel in this process. Does the message achieve the outcome you wish to accomplish? If not, place yourself in their shoes. How can this message be stated in a way that will help achieve your desired outcome? What else needs to happen or be communicated?

If the message challenges your audience, what you notice may disturb you. Feeling the fear of a group can bring up some uncomfortable feelings within you. For my staff, I knew about some of the fear going on for them, but I often pushed it aside hoping they would just get through it. In retrospect, I realize I carried judgments about their inability to manage their own fears...and their own careers, too.

Understanding how limiting decisions can affect an organization, I now realize it is most respectful for a leader to speak the fears of the people out loud. Voicing the fears gives everyone permission to face them and begin to deal with them.

STEPS TO PREPARE FOR SPEAKING TO A GROUP

1. Define or identify the message you want to deliver.

2. Ask, "What outcome do I want to create with this message?"

3. Play the communication out in your mind. Pay particular attention to the reaction of the audience. Tap into the energy of your audience to get an even better sense of how the message will be received.

4. Compare the probable reaction to the outcome you wanted to create.

5. Make any adjustments in the message based on your observations.

6. Repeat Steps 3 – 5 to check the outcome of the new message.

Looking back, if I had acknowledged the fears of my staff openly, then followed by asking simple questions to engage them in the solution, the outcome would have been better. I realize now that my audience never heard my messages of excitement about the distant opportunity. Instead, they were listening for the answer to only one question, "What actions was I taking to resolve their fears?" Checking in intuitively—going within to ask and then listen—would have put me more "in tune" with the communication needs of the group.

The sixth step is to ask, "What is my intention in delivering this message?" You can ask it at any time throughout this process. However, I place it here at the end of these steps because your message may have changed by the time you reach this point. Fully understanding your intention can help you discover any hidden agendas and prevent sending out mixed messages.

In my hard-learned lesson, had I stopped to look closely at my intentions, I would have realized I wanted the staff to get excited about the big opportunity. Yet *my* good intention was out of alignment with *their* reality. This misalignment fanned the fire of the pain and dissatisfaction instead of lessening it.

Communicating Online

If you have ever received an angry e-mail message—or one that felt like something was "up" for the sender—you have experienced blocked energy through a computer connection. Responding to such a message online rarely resolves the issue; more likely, it will make it worse.

When I receive such a message, I recognize it as a call for help, even if that is not clearly stated in the message. If I have to reply online, it will be to schedule a time to talk face-to-face or via phone so I can understand the issue(s) more fully. *This is important.*

It's easy to feel pressed for time and want to respond quickly to get the issue off your "to do" list. However, when you receive a message that gives you a strong indication something more needs to be dealt with, *listen to your inner wisdom* and respond accordingly. I have found that taking time to resolve such hunches—also called running interference— saves significant time later on.

Do you think about the energy you send along with an electronic message? The impersonal factor of the individual not being right there seems to lessen the need to think through the message or response. Even worse, it seems to give permission to speak out, saying what you would never have the courage to say directly. However, remember that thoughts are energy, too. The *energy* of the message is fully present, even if the person is not.

Use all of the techniques described here for delivering and receiving a message. If you get a message that brings up issues for you, receiving it electronically gives you the opportunity to "tune in" to any reactions that have been triggered before you decide how to respond.

When sending a message, use the same steps to formulate it as if you were going to speak to these recipients in person. Quiet your mind, center your body, and then determine what message you want to convey. Recipients will appreciate the brief time you take to do this and you'll get your messages across more clearly.

Conclusion

Certainly the right use of language and grammar helps convey any message, whether in person or in writing. However, the mindset of everyone involved in a communication factors into its successful outcome. Quieting your mind, centering your body, then taking a moment to plan the communication to match your intention and outcome takes your communication to new levels of success.

In the long run, people long for the *energetic connection*, not the content. Knowing how to deliver a clear, well-thought-out message is a gift. And to be truly *heard* is an even greater gift. Applying these deeper understandings of how good communication works makes this connection possible.

Chapter Eight
Integration: Managing Your Energy

We have looked at individual elements of how our energy interacts in the workplace. Now let's look at how we integrate all of these concepts, applying them to day-to-day challenges in the workplace.

At the core is the basic understanding that we can only manage our own energy. This was introduced in the chapter on energy. However, let me emphasize the importance of this concept. I often find that people will agree with this in theory but don't truly know what this means. So let's explore this more deeply.

The Inner Path of Work

On the surface, managing our own energy sounds simple — and in concept, it is. What makes it difficult to put into practice is the prevalent belief that we have little influence on what the external world *does* to us.

The truth is, our reactions to the external world are ours to own. We *do* have the power to choose how to respond to situations and the actions of others…*if* we commit to doing so. The key is to identify the unconscious patterns that drive us and bring them into our conscious awareness. Then we have the ability to choose our reactions.

Since work environments are so external (that is, everything is based on external actions and results), it is easy to forget to *manage our own energy.* The irony is that when we focus on what we truly *can* manage—our own thoughts and energy—our external world not only works much better, but we actually create results with greater ease and flow!

Those of us in management positions experience a constant stream of 360-degree feedback, with challenges coming from the boss, peers, and those we lead. We are often tested to the "max." Situations can trigger any unconscious thought patterns that no longer serve us. If we use these challenges and embrace what is triggered as exactly this—feedback that points us to what we need to clear within ourselves—we find we are on one of the most accelerated paths to realization on the planet. The more inner work we do, the less the external world can control us.

As mentioned in the Introduction, I had dedicated much of my personal time to exploring these concepts outside of my job. Through that effort, I came to realize the power of my own choices. Applying this in my personal life, my relationships and family matters transformed and became easier. Yet I still found it difficult to apply these concepts in my business life. Baffled by this, I decided to leave my corporate position to seek the answers away from the environment that drained me.

I soon realized why I felt such resistance: *I still wanted the organization to change.* My own judgment of how others "showed up" continued to block my own energy! This realization shifted everything. That's when I accepted this belief: My boss, my peers, my employees, and *myself* were all doing the best they could. It's a belief that's allowed me to fully *be* in the environment without being drained.

When I returned to corporate life in a management position after two years away, I had an entirely different understanding and experience. I learned to let go of those areas I couldn't change while owning those that I could. In the end, I was able to do far more with greater ease and with much less stress.

When I finally understood this paradox, I began to see how the work environment provides an extraordinary opportunity to help us identify and clear our blocks. Every external challenge that creates a reaction within us provides a profound opportunity for transformation and growth. The question remains, "Are we willing to acknowledge and accept this?"

Beyond Responsibility

Looking at my colleagues in this new light also shifted my understanding of responsibility—a major topic for the typical work environment. Manage by Objective (MBO) is a well-known concept in many organizations. Most organizations have objectives and goals defined at many levels—from individual/team objectives to department and company goals.

Employees know this routine. They are accountable for reaching their objectives by a specified time. Rewards and incentives are often attached to the timely achievement of stated objectives. This is appropriate use of personal energy. As described in the chapters on Intention and Commitment, it takes aligned intention and commitment at the individual level for objectives to become reality.

Most people accept the responsibility of achieving key objectives. As one advances, responsibility broadens and learning to delegate tasks becomes essential. Yet, sometimes the need to achieve gets confused with taking responsibility for areas that energetically we can't be responsible for. And even those who are good at delegation may not fully understand how to manage the energetic accountability that goes with the activity being delegated.

This concept never entered into my mind before I became aware of my own energy field or the energy of others. It never dawned on me that my energy might have been extended in areas that did not serve others or myself. Typically, I would take on any challenge that walked into my office. Saying "no" to something rarely occurred to me. But more importantly, I felt it was my job to take on whatever was put in front of me.

In my early career, it was exciting to feel I could conquer any situation that was posed to me. My desire to help and/or "fix" the situation got me involved in all kinds of activities that weren't necessarily part of my stated objectives. I thought that was all normal and part of my job—especially as a manager. After all, it seemed to accelerate my career advancement. However, it did not take long before I was overextended, mostly because I would take on responsibilities that belonged to someone else rather than facilitate that individual toward a solution he or she owned.

As my awareness grew, I paid attention to situations in which my energy plummeted. I was surprised to find myself especially drained at times I thought I was helping others! Using the process to uncover intention (described in the chapter on intention), I was able to uncover my unconscious intention: to alter or control the outcome, even if the responsibility for that belonged to the other person.

Many times, my need to intervene in a situation extended to my peers or even my boss. Of course, I was well meaning and believed helping was essential to having a successful career. However, once I realized I could not manage the energy of another person, I began to understand the absurdity of what I was trying to do. Digging deeper, I always found I had an agenda to "fix" the other person or situation. The question then became, "How do I shift this?"

What Is Mine To Do?

The answer lay in this simple question, "What is mine to do?" This is one of the most useful tools I've found to help me remember to manage *my* energy, not others. No matter how complicated the situation or how much pressure I'd feel to take on the responsibility of another, I'd stop and ask: "What is mine to do in this situation? What role do I need to play with this individual?"

I introduced this question in the chapter on intuition, for it's best to first quiet the mind and center the body before asking the question. This helps get to the *real* answer versus a rationalized answer based on "what should be."

Several years ago, when I was a senior manager responsible for the majority of operations for a service organization, an employee approached me about a problem she was having with a colleague. It seems that her colleague frequently made errors that she was noticing. Feeling like this colleague was reflecting poorly on the performance of their team, she wanted me to know who was the source of the errors. In addition, this situation was stressing her to the point of affecting her work.

Now, in the organization, this employee didn't report directly to me but reported to one of my managers. So by virtue of the reporting relationship alone, dealing with this issue was *not* mine to do. In my early career, I would commonly intervene, possibly interfering with or overriding the responsibilities of my manager. Now, having a different perspective, I proceeded carefully.

I was already aware of corrective action being taken by the manager to address this issue. Because of this, I asked her the obvious question, "Have you brought this to the attention of your manager?" The answer was "kind of." I soon learned of some issues she had with her boss, including judgments she held about his competence. By coming to me, she was hoping I would "fix" more than one area—both her boss and her colleague.

When I asked myself, "What was mine to do?" I realized I had to support this employee in owning her part in all of this. First I explained that both her manager and myself were aware of the source of the errors and corrective action was in process. I assured her that her own performance was not jeopardized because of these issues.

As I attempted to assure her, it was clear (by observing and sensing her energy) that this issue was not resolved from her standpoint. I almost anticipated this as I closely observed her through the conversation. But I knew it was important to address the issue she brought to the table, first.

So the next question I asked her was, "What did she want me to do with this information?" This led her to look at her own attachment to having things resolved *her way*. She clearly wanted me to manage the energy of two other people—perhaps even punish them in some way. So, I asked her, "What do you want me to say to your manager concerning this situation?" Thinking this through, she said she really didn't want it known that she had come to me. She said she *had* brought this to his attention and he had made some improvements, but not to the level she wanted or at the speed she wanted.

I continued to ask questions to identify the source of her issues with her boss. She admitted she had decided he was not fixing the problems fast enough for her. Also, she held high expectations of her other colleagues, expecting them to work up to her standards. Then we moved on to talk about her stress.

Clearly, this individual was worrying about something that was not *hers* to do. Taking on the responsibility of her colleague's performance (and also, to some extent, her manager's performance) wasn't her job. All of this worrying increased her stress. So I asked her if she had ever been able to *make* someone do something—including her children? She laughed and said, "No, not really." "Well," I replied, "neither have I!"

We talked about the concept of only managing *her* energy— not everybody else's. It was a radical idea for her. I coached her to look at the source of her stress. Worrying about how others "show up" (or don't show up) is a sure formula for stress. She realized she could be far more productive and less stressed by focusing on only what's hers to do.

A year later, she told me how helpful that coaching session was. Until then, she had no idea how much energy she expended managing everyone else (including her spouse and children), and how little she had left for herself. She was still working on managing her expectations of others, but she clearly had reduced her stress levels by paying more attention to where she placed her energy.

Taking Responsibility

The flip side of taking on responsibility that is *not* mine to do is *not* taking responsibility for what does belong to you.

Of course, we have all seen the victim scenario when someone blames others for external factors one can't control, while not owning the decisions and actions they *do* control. However, like the example of my employee, a subtler pattern occurs when people take on the actions of others while not owning the part that belongs to them.

As with any unconscious thought pattern, people may not even realize they aren't "owning" what is theirs. Think about the example above when the employee tried to take on responsibility that wasn't hers, yet didn't focus on the part that clearly belonged to her. She believed her colleague was causing her stress. More accurately, she caused herself stress by focusing on the part she couldn't manage while ignoring the part she could — her reaction to her colleague.

Over the years, I rarely thought of myself as a victim; indeed, I would err on the side of taking on responsibility that wasn't mine. However, I began to realize that, just like my employee, I began to resent certain situations — ones in which I allowed myself to take on what belonged to other people.

Several years ago, I had a boss who disliked dealing with certain conflict situations. Because I had a reputation of being good at turning around such situations, he'd often delegate these issues to me. For the most part, I didn't mind being asked to help out. I rather enjoyed being respected for my facilitation ability.

However, as time went on, I recognized that my boss often played a part in setting up the conflicts within our department. He developed a bad reputation for getting different people in our department off on tangents that caused confusion and conflict among them. And I was getting known for cleaning up after him.

One day, he asked me to resolve a conflict between two of my peers. As usual, I accepted the challenge but I could feel resentment building. Discovering he had again played a role in creating this conflict, I faced another situation of cleaning it up for him. I finally became aware that I was falling into a pattern of taking care of situations that really belonged to him—not me.

When I asked the question, "What is mine to do?" the answer came back right away. I had to tell my boss the truth and support him in participating in the solution. Ultimately, I had to coach him to find ways to prevent similar situations. I held this as my intention and set out to accomplish it.

First, I did some assessments with the people involved before I went back to my boss. I suspected he was running on a deeper intention that I didn't understand. Realizing this, I prepared to use the PROCESS TO UNCOVER ACTUAL INTENT described in the Intention chapter.

When I first broached the topic with my boss, he was annoyed that I didn't just "handle it." But I carefully stated the issue, including what impact this action was having on the group. He slowly opened up and admitted his impatience with certain behaviors. To counter this, he would "stir things up," getting several different actions going for the same requirement. He wanted to see who could get the task done first, rationalizing that "a little competition was a good thing!"

Now that I understood his deeper intention for doing this, I asked him to look at how others might view this. I asked how he might feel if someone did this to him. Slowly he began to understand the negative consequences of his actions. We talked about the amount of energy this took away from the goals we needed to achieve as a group. Now that he understood the impact to the bottom line, we talked about what his actions were doing to his reputation. He acknowledged this was not an outcome he wanted.

That led to a conversation about how he might achieve the outcome he originally wanted — getting his team in action quickly — without sending them in different directions. We brainstormed several possibilities, making sure each option would work for him. This is a key point. So often we try to help by offering options that might work for us, but they won't necessarily work for those who need them. Asking what they might do differently is the key. Another approach is to offer an idea and then ask if that might work them. Let *them* own the solution. It goes back to first owning the intention and commitment to create the result that works uniquely for them.

My boss and I continued to brainstorm the best way to correct the conflicts that prompted our conversation. He decided he would talk to each person individually, explaining his realization and helping reset priorities in a way that would complement each other's actions, not conflict with them. Needless to say, the two individuals were amazed and grateful. The entire team (and department) benefited from the shift in our boss's behavior. It didn't take long for the word to get out that something changed for the better.

The benefit to me was that I stopped enabling situations that clearly belonged to my boss. In addition, I earned his respect and turned around a pattern that could have led to loss of respect for him. It would not have taken much for my resentment to build up to total disrespect for him.

Now, when I'm approached to do something that is not on my plan, I ask, "What is mine to do in this situation?" The answer will often be to guide or coach rather than do or control — and I have learned the subtle but important difference between them. Yet, sometimes the answer comes back that this situation is clearly *not* mine to do; instead, it may hold important lessons for the other participants.

It is important for me not to take someone else's learning away by intervening where I'm not really needed. Helping responsible people out when they get stuck is teamwork; repeatedly rescuing someone is not. In fact, it can take away the individual's lesson while draining your own energy. Knowing when to intervene — and when not to — can free up enormous amounts of energy that can be used to support objectives that truly belong to you.

Learning to Tell The Truth

After reading this story, you might say, "Facing *my* boss on something like this is certainly *not* mine to do!" Yet I would pose these questions back: "How many times do we enable someone around us to continue a limiting pattern that clearly wastes or drains energy in our work group without ever approaching that person to find out the true motivation? How many times are we afraid to tell the truth and give real feedback (feedback that includes the impact that his or her actions are creating for the group) to a boss, peer, or co-worker?"

Telling the truth can be considered the same as "not lying." Of course, since lying is "bad," we all should simply tell the truth — right? But it's not that simple. Certainly lying is not a good thing, yet telling the truth often means, "being in touch with what's in the realm of unconscious thought patterns." Denial, unconscious thoughts patterns, and long-held beliefs about what might happen if the truth is revealed, all stand in the way of getting the truth on the table.

Telling the truth takes both courage and compassion. This applies whether you are facing the truth about yourself or giving constructive feedback to someone else.

Identifying what's at the heart of a matter for you is the first step toward becoming better at telling the truth to others. Taking time to quiet the mind and center the body provides the setting to go within and find the answers to what is true for you. Once you are aware of what you feel and know, you are better prepared to look at the truth about whatever external situation stands before you.

When telling others the truth, it takes courage to rise above the fears of the consequences we may face as a result of telling someone what we truly feel. But, more importantly, it takes moving past our blocks and judgments to be open and compassionate enough to realize how others appear to us maybe outside of their conscious awareness. Therefore, giving feedback may trigger negative reactions in them.

This section is labeled "Learning to Tell the Truth" because my experience – both in my own career and with clients – tells me that few people really know how to do this. Along with the fears of the consequences one might face by telling someone the truth, I often hear, "telling the truth might hurt the individual." Because there is so much conditioning to withhold truthful feedback, few have learned to do it well.

Courage and compassion actually go hand-in-hand. Identifying and addressing your own issues first clears the way, building courage for the action to take place. In the example of my boss, I first had to get past my judgments that "he should know better than to create conflicts in his own organization." I also had to face the fact that I had *agreed* to resolve his conflicts, enabling a pattern I now had to face myself. At the core was facing my own truth first and then owning what was mine.

Often, when giving feedback, we simply want to call out what *we* see is the deeper intention that is unconscious for the individual. Knowing that an *unconscious* intention is overriding the action helps a person shift from the need to tell the truth, to a process that helps the individual uncover his or her blind spot. Getting to this realization makes the probing conversation much easier. For example, with my boss, my goal was to listen to his side of "why he did this" versus wanting to make him wrong.

Steps to Telling the Truth

So here are some simple steps to follow when giving good feedback or telling someone the truth about a difficult matter.

First, identify any judgments you're holding or limiting decisions you've made about this individual (or situation). One way is to imagine yourself giving the feedback and notice any reactions or resistance that come up.

Then follow these triggers to the source of the reaction. Tell yourself the truth about what decisions you have made concerning this situation. Use the PROCESS TO IDENTIFY AND CLEAR UNCONSCIOUS THOUGHT PATTERNS defined in the Energy chapter.

Clear any judgment by holding the possibility that you really don't know what this behavior or action does for this individual. Similarly, you don't know that this individual truly doesn't understand the impact of his or her actions. Since this is probably a blind spot for this person, it's highly probable this is the truth anyway.

After clearing any judgments, repeat the first step, once again imagining yourself giving the feedback. If you have done your homework, you should notice it's much easier and the resistance will be lessened or gone. If resistance still exists, follow it back to the source and repeat the process again.

Finally, take a moment to identify any role you might have played in the situation. Tell yourself the truth of what you own in the process. Even if you don't share this information with the person involved, it still helps free your energy. In the case of my boss, it was helpful to acknowledge that I'd agreed to resolve conflicts in the past, but then I realized it wasn't helping him or the organization in the long run. Sharing this helped him understand why I had a change of heart.

When it's time to actually deliver the message, take a moment to center yourself. During the conversation, listen carefully to the person's response. Listen for the "why" behind the actions. Then help the person understand the affect his or her particular behavior is having.

PREPARATION FOR DELIVERING FEEDBACK

1. **Imagine actually delivering the feedback to the individual(s). Notice if it brings up any reaction within you.**

2. **Identify and clear any judgments or limiting decisions about the individual(s) or situation. Use the PROCESS TO IDENTIFY AND CLEAR UNCONSCIOUS THOUGHT PATTERNS (see Energy: The Source).**

3. **Repeat Steps 1and 2 until you feel your energy is clear of blocks.**

4. **If applicable, identify any role you might have played in the situation.**

5. **When it's time to deliver the feedback, take the time to quiet your mind and center your body.**

Finally, now that you understand the actual situation, brainstorm alternatives that will work *for the individual*. Remember, the intention and commitment that will create a new outcome belongs to him or her, not you.

Embrace the Learning

Realizing that people in any organization come to work with unresolved emotional blocks, is it any wonder that issues surface and play out in the workplace?

The work environment provides opportunities for growth just as families and relationships outside of work do, too. Yet, many people leave family situations or relationships hoping they'll find something or someone better without looking at what role they might have played. The same scenario can happen on the work front when someone views the organization as "dysfunctional" and tries to leave the position without stopping to embrace the learning. Ironically, that person often attracts the same situation in their next place of work.

Along with my experience of leaving an organization prematurely (which I shared in Integrity: The Journey to Wholeness), I have coached many who wanted to leave their current work situation to find something better or to just get out of a "bad" situation. In the "bad" situation, frequently the individuals have not looked at what role they played nor asked themselves: "Why have they brought this experience into their life?" Exploring these questions can shift their perspective quickly. But sometimes the person may have the best intentions for leaving and still has some learning to complete before moving on to the next opportunity.

When the desired position doesn't show up, no matter how much effort they put into it, I ask, "What do you have to learn from the current situation?" This is not a popular question but when the individual faces this answer, it provides a profound learning. It's a lesson that they had to embrace before they left or they would have re-created it in the next position they found.

Example Situation

A few years ago a colleague was ready to move on to a new opportunity. She had been leading a complex project that was coming to a successful close. Having been in this organization for many years, she had served in several management roles and achieved many accomplishments. This latest project would be hard to top in terms of additional growth. So feeling complete with what she had accomplished, she got ready to move on.

Having a particular timeframe in mind, she was doing all of the right things to land a new position. She had carefully thought through what she wanted and targeted appropriately. Her resume was in order, she researched companies that looked promising, and she was working all of her contacts in her network. Yet, despite all of her efforts, nothing was showing up.

One day, she relayed her disappointment about her situation to me. She asked me to check in with my intuition and see if I got any insights of what she needed to do differently. I immediately received a sense of conflict she hadn't told me about. So I asked her if there was some issue she was having with anyone in the organization. She described a situation with a new senior manager who had just arrived in her department.

She began to describe how annoyed she was with his incompetence. She could see how much of the groundwork that she had so carefully laid—in building a successful team and implementing processes—could easily be destroyed after she left. To complete her major project, she was to transition her project team into an ongoing support function that would report to this new manager. Rarely did they talk, so she was deeply concerned about his ability to maintain this group well.

At first, she could not believe there could be a correlation between the "stuff" she was dealing with in her current situation and her finding a new position. In fact, it seemed even more important to leave now because it was clear that upper management didn't understand (let alone value) the work she'd accomplished. So she wanted out—as soon as possible.

Together we identified two areas that energetically held her where she was. The first was her judgment about this new manager and the second was her attachment to having the organization be maintained at the level she created while she was there.

I supported her in clearing her judgment, which in turn helped her look at this individual differently. As part of the intuitive insight, I realized this person was actually threatened by my colleague because she has been extremely successful and emits an air of confidence. Again, it was hard for my friend to believe she frightened this guy, but she made some changes. Somewhat humoring me, she dropped the judgment she held and softened her approach to him.

To her amazement, her relationship with this individual changed immediately. She realized how her own judgment sent out an energetic message that heightened his feeling of being threatened. This individual knew it wasn't going to be easy to follow in her footsteps. He began to ask her questions and involve her in brainstorming to determine how best to transition her project team—none of which happened before she dropped her judgment and approached him openly.

Her second challenge was letting go of how the organization would continue, including feeling responsible for her team. It was important to understand that those who stay behind choose to do so. They'll have their own growth opportunities as a result. Trying to hold on to what might have been would only have drained her energy.

In this example, my colleague was ready to move on for good reasons, yet she unknowingly blocked the possibilities until she uncovered the learning she still needed before she found her next position. So often, those who just want to leave cite lots of external evidence about the organization being dysfunctional. Illogical as it may seem, taking time to look within and ask, "What do I have to learn from this situation?" is the very ticket to moving on to the next opportunity.

Stress from an Energy Perspective

A chapter on managing your energy would not be complete without looking at the topic of stress from the perspective of personal energy.

Considering the pace of the world we live in, dealing with stress is a frequent complaint. We might associate a major component of stress with the demands of our job, but it is often compounded by stress caused by the needs of home and family. Balancing these areas challenges many.

In a simpler time, we had fewer choices to make concerning where to focus our attention. Today, our world provides a limitless number of options (also seen as demands) that vie for the same amount of energy we had when the world was much simpler. In days gone by, there were fewer pressures, so learning how to use our personal energy was not even on our scope. But today is a different story. To regain the natural flow we have as our birthright, it's important to understand how each of us contributes to the stress in our lives.

There are plenty of techniques and courses on how to manage time and finances, yet how often do we pay attention to how we manage our own energy? We probably make more choices about how we spend our money then how we use our precious energy. Nowhere do we learn how to remain in a state of flow, moving from task to activity totally stress free. To compound the issue, most of us have been conditioned that adding to our energetic burden is good; it's something that will get us what we want in life. Unfortunately, this has helped create the out of balance condition so many face today. So letting go of the old way and paying attention to where and how we use our personal energy is at the heart of the solution.

Throughout this chapter, I have touched on situations that cause stress. Trying to be responsible for others and for areas we have no control over are examples of how stress sets up energetically. In the example of my employee who was stressed by the actions of her colleague, we recognized her belief that her stress was caused by something outside of her control. In fact, she caused it by misplaced use of her own energy.

Once again, shifting from a belief that something *external* causes our stress to accepting that *our own thoughts and choices* play a significant role is critical to alleviating stress in our lives. Be willing to ask yourself, "What role am I playing in creating this stress that I am feeling?" Then pay attention to the answer. This can do wonders to shift any resistance you feel.

One stress-creating pattern I discovered when I asked myself this question was that I'd constantly tell myself, "I don't have enough time." This insidious little phase carries the power to stress me out—and it can totally slip by my conscious awareness. If you say it too, you can rationalize that, after all, when you combine all of the deadlines you face, there isn't enough time, right? Well, maybe.

As tasks and deadlines pile up, we don't stop to sort out what we need to do differently. Instead, we tend to continue pushing through, all the time knowing (often at an unconscious level) we aren't going to make it. The "knowing we aren't going to make it" actually sets up the stress.

I finally discovered the power of the thought "I don't have enough time" when I got stressed over some deadlines that were totally of my making. Feeling the stress, I finally stopped and asked, "What is the source of this stress?" Realizing I had begun this new project feeling I wouldn't have time to fit it into my busy schedule, I stepped back and reevaluated what I had to accomplish. In this particular case, I decided not to change the due date but to change my belief about the project. I began by saying, "I have the time I need to accomplish this." To my amazement, the task flowed and I was able to complete it in the time I had allotted. Most importantly, the stress was gone!

Ways to Reduce Stress

Having looked at our core belief concerning the source of our stress, let's address three areas that will make a significant impact in reducing stress. They are: (1) identifying and clearing the limiting thought patterns that restrict energy flow; (2) looking at the choices we make in how we use our energy; and, (3) maintaining a quiet mind and centered state.

Throughout this book, we've looked at the significance of limiting thought patterns and how they block energy. It stands to reason that any restriction of our subtle energy drains our energy. So do the strategies we have learned to combat or work around them. Many of the self-help techniques we rely on temporarily fix the symptoms caused by blocks, but they rarely address the core issue. Since the core issue remains, one must continue to apply certain techniques to keep the symptoms at bay—and this takes energy.

When we fully address a core issue, though—identifying the source of the block and clearing it—we immediately have more energy. Often after such a clearing, I hear the remark, "I had no idea just how much that (issue) was draining me!" So once again, I emphasize the importance of identifying limiting thought patterns and clearing them.

Some limiting thought patterns might not appear to be major. In fact, certain ones produce stress as the main trigger. A common example occurs when we spend a lot of time and energy thinking about what we "should have done" or "what should be." We definitely spend precious personal energy concerned about something out of our control or influence. This can be a tremendous energy drain, equating to lots of self-induced stress.

The best cure for this is to stop the moment you notice you are saying or thinking something *should* be different. Take a moment to reflect on this statement, "It is as it is." Then, with a clear and calm mind, ask, "What is mine to do in this situation?" From this centered place, you can focus on what is the best course of action and your role in it. Of course, the answer may be "there is nothing to do." If this is the case, acknowledge it as truth and let it go! Just breathe deeply and feel your energy open and your stress dissolve as you embrace this.

This brings us to the second area: being conscious of how we *choose* to use our energy. We have taken a look at how identifying, "What is mine to do?" can help redirect personal energy flow. Paying attention to times when we feel resistance or when something feels hard to do signals that we're expending energy in areas that aren't appropriate. The key is to ask this question at the first sign of resistance.

The third area is maintaining a quiet mind and centered state. Using the exercises described in the chapter on integrity regularly can help you maintain a calm state. It is in a centered state that choices are much clearer and easier to make, especially when considering, "What is mine to do?" It is also a prerequisite to obtaining clearer information from your intuition.

WAYS TO REDUCE STRESS

1. **Identify and clear any limiting thought patterns that are restricting your energy flow.**

2. **Make conscious choices in how you use your energy. Especially pay attention to, "what is yours to do?"**

3. **Maintain a quiet mind and centered state.**

You may already use physical techniques such as yoga or exercise to help shift from a stressful to calm state. Just about any physical activity (even getting up and taking a quick break) can stop stress temporarily. The three areas outlined above focus on getting to the source of the stress; exercise can certainly help to augment these areas. Personally, I have gained greater benefit from every activity and enjoy life much more as I pursue my inner work.

Key to Integration

Once we begin to realize we can only manage our own thoughts, our own energy, and our own reactions to others, the whole world changes around us. Embracing this concept is the key to integrating energy into our daily work life.

Looking at the corporate world with a mechanistic view, we often see dysfunction and an organization we want to change, a place where we want the top executives to "just get it" and make it better.

Looking at that same world through the eyes of one on an inner journey, we see the collective energy of individuals doing the best they can—working through the unconscious thought patterns that drive them. Looking closer, we can see the resistance and flow as individuals play out the consequences of their choices (both conscious and unconscious).

From this understanding, it is possible to *be* in what often appears as chaos instead of resisting it or trying to change it. It is from this place that peace is regained.

The paradox is that from a place of "being" we actually *can* change the organization. Ironically, it is not because we set out to change it; it changes because of the extraordinary potential that is unleashed as people take back what is theirs— understanding the power of who they really are.

Chapter Nine
Leadership: The New Role

Throughout this book, I have shared examples of how my own view of being a leader changed as I came to better understand the unseen energies within myself, as well as the collective energy of each group I managed.

Over time, it became clear that I could lead others, but it was their choice to follow. I could guide or teach others, but it was their choice to learn. Most importantly, I realized that, to fully *manage* the tasks and milestones of a group, I had to work with the key individuals and clearly communicate the requirements. I also had to help them build their own intentions and commitment to create the end result. These realizations allowed me to shift from a "command and control" style to guiding and facilitating the required outcomes.

I have used the words "manager" and "leader" interchangeably many times in this material. In the past, I would have made specific distinctions between the two, sighting that managers focus on managing the tactics in an organization while leaders focus on vision and direction. The

147

analogy I've often used is: while managers place the ladder up against a house and supervise the repairs, the leader decides which house to work on.

Today, the need to do both—that is, lead direction and manage tactics—certainly has not gone away. As we deal with the incredible amount and pace of change, managers must be leaders. More importantly, leadership skills will be required throughout the ranks of an organization. In essence, it already is a requirement; however, it is not always recognized as such. As complexity increases, each person in an organization must be able to rise to the leadership challenges of the specific needs of their functional area. At the same time, individuals must learn to manage their own energy.

So the question remains, "If we can only manage our own energy, what is the true role of a manager or leader?"

Aligning for Results

For leaders at the top of organizations, defining and communicating clear vision, mission, and strategy is more important than ever before. The challenges come when strategies (and at times even vision and mission) change due to the reality of keeping up with an ever-changing marketplace. Making sure course corrections are rapidly implemented can be critical for the survival of a company.

Rapid implementation means getting everyone on the same page—now! Therefore, leaders and managers within the organization are finding themselves in a new role supporting this continual effort of realignment. These middle managers must understand the vision, mission, and strategy clearly enough not only speak it, but to *model* it. In addition, applying the concept, "you can only manage your energy" requires managers to guide the organization in the creation of aligned intention and commitment energy.

All of this must happen within a short period of time so their employees can align and become productive as quickly as possible. Again, without this realignment, change efforts often fail to bring about the promised result that started the organization down this path in the first place.

Unfortunately, managers often end up having to communicate new direction to employees with little (or no) time to fully internalize the change themselves. Allowing middle managers to internalize what this change means for them becomes a critical success factor, for it provides the inner alignment necessary to communicate the change to the next level with congruence.

To accomplish this, managers need to go through the process described in the chapter on commitment (ALIGNING INTENTION AND COMMITMENT FOR CHANGE) first. Once they understand the change, they are then prepared to facilitate the same process with their staff. This allows employees to internalize the change enough so they, too, can set their own intention and commitment energies in motion.

Facilitating Versus Managing

The process to guide group alignment (ALIGNING INTENTION AND COMMITMENT FOR CHANGE) is just one of many examples of facilitated processes in this book. This is an especially important shift for managers and leaders to make — *to manage less and facilitate more.*

I've shared stories of my own shift as my awareness opened. When I look back, I see the biggest outward change in my leadership style was to move from directing and managing to coaching and facilitating. This is not to say that directing or managing should completely go away. However, the need exists to *balance* these options with an ability to facilitate an individual or group and to coach others to manage their energy. *This cannot be accomplished by telling them what to do.* Rather, it takes guiding them to find the answers within themselves. This is true empowerment.

Over the last ten years, I've seen organizations attempt to build coaching skills into their management and/or leadership competencies. This is a sign that the need has been identified and certainly is a great start. However, in my experience, that's not an easy transition to make. I believe the reason for this difficulty lies in the fact that coaching is not a skill per se. Certainly, people can learn certain questioning frameworks and coaching processes. However, at the core of a good (or great) coach or facilitator is ongoing dedication to one's inner work. This provides the greatest insights in guiding others to do the same, for the true coach helps them find answers within versus telling them the recommended approach.

Thus, change in the inner mindset is at the heart of opening to one's coaching ability. This, of course, cannot be taught through traditional skills training. Those who attempt to use coaching frameworks without checking in to identify any decisions or judgments they hold about the person cannot coach. Why? Because their unconscious thoughts will come through to the individual. As a result, that person won't feel safe or gain value from the process. Let's look at a simple example.

At the core of good coaching and facilitation is the ability to ask questions that help another person discover answers and identify solutions that works. When supporting managers in coaching others, I often uncover situations in which the manager had difficulties asking good questions. In one specific situation, I was working in an organization that was rolling out coaching as a requirement for their sales managers. One sales manager was having difficulty with a new member of his sales team. Specifically, the manager was trying to help him shift his behavior when it came to following through on sales leads.

I asked him to describe how he had coached his junior sales team member so far. Along with the standard sales targets, he had worked with this sales representative to develop goals for the number of calls made. He suggested several strategies that might help improve his follow through. After several failed attempts, he resorted to a more standard approach: a warning.

I asked the sales manager if he had ever asked his subordinate what stopped him from meeting his goals? Or what could he do differently to meet the goals? The answer was, "No." Now coaching the sales manager, I asked, "What stopped you from asking these questions?" His reply was very telling: "I believe he should have gotten these ideas by now! After all, it's a basic sales requirement."

Even as he said the words, the sales manager "got" that his own judgment was in the way. Changing his decision, he began a new approach. He was able to support his salesperson in discovering what unconscious thought pattern got in the way of successfully meeting his goals. With this discovery, the sales representative was able to see what ultimately prevented him from obtaining his sales targets.

This speaks to the importance of a manager or leader to look within before guiding others. Only those who have faced and now know their own inner map can truly help others find solutions that work for them.

Developing the Leader Within

The time is upon us. The number of challenges in organizations has escalated to levels we never thought possible. Recognizing that things need to be different, some organizations have identified new leadership competencies and defined the latest capabilities one must have to meet the challenge. Often, these definitions are stated in terms of what a leader must demonstrate outwardly.

As noted in the Introduction, the answer lies not in what leaders have to do differently but in what they must become. This shift is possible when people augment their business skills and experiences with exploration of their inner beings. This winning combination will provide the leadership needed to face today's challenges.

From the current business perspective, this may seem like a tough requirement to implement. After all, how would one identify or measure whether a person is maintaining a centered presence, owning their intentions, or creating a safe space? Attempts are made to define leadership competencies stating the outward results that these inner states may yield. Yet, often we believe one either has this inner presence or doesn't have it. Rarely is there guidance to learn how to acquire it.

Traditionally, this development of "the leader within" has occurred through the long road of life experience. Failure and disappointment, balanced by success, has been the road taken to reach the inner knowing about oneself. However, today, time is of the essence. In the hectic pace of our current world, we have so little time to reflect and learn from our experiences.

Yet, learning to remain in one's center—own one's thoughts, words, and actions (just to name a few)—and stay in the flow may already be critical requirements for a leader to be successful. Certainly if not recognized as a requirement by business, these are requirements to return the sanity and balance of life that's been lost along the way. Those who commit to their own inner work will certainly reap the benefits.

Permission for Everyone to be a Leader

I once believed that if the leaders in an organization changed, corporate America would be a much better place to work. Certainly it is true that executives who open to their inner awareness will help create a culture in which employees will want to work. Yet now I realize everyone plays a part in the collective energy of an organization. Each person who begins to take responsibility for his or her energy creates a possibility for others to do the same—thus making it a better place to work.

Extraordinary things can happen when people awaken to their own inner beings, accepting that only *they* can manage their own energy. As I was completing this material, the following remarkable story was unfolding.

While sharing the essence of this work with a good friend, he realized some areas were definite triggers for him, usually bringing up an angry response to the person who triggered him. While I supported him in identifying the source of the triggers, he traced the pattern back to decisions he made as a boy. He grew up dealing with a strict father who returned from World War II with emotional issues of his own. Early in his childhood, he had learned to defend himself by using verbal retorts to throw others off center, sometimes before they could do the same to him. He suddenly saw how he was reenacting this in several areas of his life.

At the time he uncovered these patterns, he was coordinating the renovation of a commercial building. Being in the construction business for over 30 years, he had come to accept that the typical job site provides ample opportunities for peoples' "stuff" to show up, including his. It was all part of the job—something he took for granted.

However, now having made a profound discovery about his own emotional triggers and conditioned behavior, he suddenly realized what belonged to him (emotionally) and what did not. So he began to apply his new understanding at the job site. Only a couple of days after he had begun this journey into his inner world, a whole new external world opened up for him. Excited, he called me to share the miracles that were happening on the job!

He said he began to understand the power his energy had in creating a smooth and safe place to work. With many of his triggers gone, others responded to him in remarkable ways because they recognized he was much easier to talk to. He also realized how his past judgments of certain people contributed to the difficulties he'd had with them. Aware of those judgments and now able to make a new choice about each person he had judged in the past, he began to understand the dynamics that caused them to respond to him the way they did.

About three months into his new awareness, I requested an in-depth conversation about his breakthrough. When I asked him what benefits he experienced from the shift he'd made, he immediately said, "I listen more." He explained that since his main triggers were essentially gone and he no longer triggered others, his communication had improved dramatically. He said: "The more I listen, the more information I receive. The more information I receive, the better I am at responding to the issue at hand." He spoke of the overall impact it had on other contractors by saying: "As my communication improved, people opened up. When people are open in this way, there is more productivity on the job."

He also noticed how his intuition naturally opened. He began to "just know" or anticipate what was needed or what was about to happen. "The big picture of what was needed for a given day," became apparent to him. He remarked about his ability to center and quiet his mind, something that was almost impossible before. If things got off on a bad start due to external circumstances, he was able to "restart the day" by taking a moment to stop and breathe.

Having read through much of this manuscript, he was especially intrigued by the power intention plays in creating results. He realized another trigger for him occurred when he knew "in his heart of hearts" that a particular person wasn't going to "show up" or deliver what was promised. Before he understood the importance of intention, he would continue to be disappointed time after time because he'd been trying to get a blocked individual to commit to a particular outcome.

When he shifted to discernment, he realized that, in these situations, the individual never *intended* to show up. Clearing his past resentment and shifting to a conversation about the real issue—the person's intention—he was able to help that person set realistic deadlines that worked for both of them.

In the past, he had tried to change his style of communicating and leading others, but he was never able to sustain it. Now, as a result of identifying and clearing the unconscious patterns that drove him, he did not have to think about what to do or say differently; the words just came from his heart. The impact on the job included saving enormous amounts of time and energy, plus avoiding costly rework. For his own health, his stress lowered because things went more smoothly on the job. But most important, he expressed a newfound sense of peace and happiness that had eluded him in the past.

All of this was amazing. Yet the conversation didn't end there!

A Gift for Others

My friend went on to explain how he was sharing his new insights with several others—teaching them to manage their energy as well. One particular incident involved a contractor on his job. This contractor was discussing some challenges he has having on another jobsite with the office manager who approved his work. This woman was negative and impossible to please. And because they worked in tight quarters, the contractor had to be in the presence of her energy continually. He dreaded every time he had to go to that office to work.

Listening to the contractor's situation, my friend asked him, "What thoughts do *you* hold about this office manager when you work there?" Without hesitation he responded, "I hate working in her presence. She is so negative!"

My friend explained to the contractor the power his thoughts might be having on this individual. "Now, this person certainly has her own stuff to deal with, but it can't hurt to make a new decision and shift your thoughts when you approach that job site!"

The contractor took my friend's advice and changed his thoughts while at that jobsite. Days later, he returned totally excited by results that came from simply making a new decision. Working in the presence of this woman, he had a day like no other. They actually had a friendly conversation. He felt much more productive and definitely less drained. He explained: "I'm convinced! From now on I'm going to pay more attention to what thoughts I'm holding about someone I'm working around."

All of the changes that occurred in my friend's work environment as result of his dedication to manage his own energy were remarkable in themselves. But the best parts were the profound changes that happened between him and his son.

The Best Part

The divorced father of a 15 year old, he primarily saw his son on weekends. He felt good about his relationship with his son, but, like many fathers of teen-aged boys, he'd say, "They had their moments."

Now, having released the unconscious patterns that had been created in his early relationship with his own father, he could see how he was repeating similar patterns. Catching himself during an angry interlude with his son, he stopped and realized the negative impact he was having on his own child.

To his son's amazement, he apologized and began to share what he had learned about his behavior. He explained that he had identified the source of his anger from his childhood and wanted to make a new choice in how he related to his son. Over time, he shared with his son what he was learning about managing his energy and how he couldn't manage the energy of others.

I had the privilege of asking his son what was different. He told me that his father no longer reacts with anger if he *pushes* one of his dad's trigger points. "He stops and thinks things through, so we can talk." He, too, recognized that his father listened more and asked more thoughtful questions. Both of them agreed they were beginning to know each other better; building a relationship they'd never thought possible.

His son shared that he was learning to manage his own energy, too. Even with his friends and his mom, he was recognizing when he triggered something that he didn't mean to. He also began to recognize when another person was projecting something on him. In the past, he had taken certain things personally, a pattern he'd learned to protect himself. Now he can better discern what belongs to other people and not get "hooked" into their anger or emotion.

This example shows how one individual's commitment to look within positively influenced many people in his life. How many more lives might be transformed as a result of what opened for my friend? We may never know. His is a powerful example of just how much we *can* change the world around us — creating results we may not have thought possible. Imagine what could happen in any organization if even a few individuals opened to the power within themselves. This is leadership at its best — a leadership we all need to embrace.

Each of us has a choice. We can wait for those we view as leaders to embrace their inner being and guide us to this new world. Or we can choose to own it — now. Certainly the example described by my friend illustrates the benefits that await those who choose to look within.

It takes inner strength, courage, and conviction to look within — and to own the thoughts, words, and actions we put out into the world. There is a natural leader waiting to emerge in each one of us.

Each person who risks and takes this step makes it easier for the next person — and brings the organization one step closer to a new era.

About the Author

Carol Bergmann is an executive coach, facilitator and speaker. She began her professional career as a software engineer in the computer field. She has over 28 years of business experience spanning a unique combination of Information Technology, Quality Management, Business Management, and Human Resource Development.

However, the author's business experience only tells half the story. It is her dedication to her own personal growth and deep exploration of the unseen world of energy that has allowed her to bring *Managing Your Energy At Work* to life.

Since the early '80s her path has taken her into the study of Eastern philosophies, including meditation and yoga. She worked with various teachers to develop her intuitive abilities and learn to work with subtle energy fields. Since 1993 she has been applying these concepts in her business environment with remarkable results.

Most recently she founded Aligned For Action, LLC, a unique organization supporting those that seek to integrate inner wisdom into the business world. Coaching, facilitation (individual and group) and seminars are among the many services provided for those who dare to step outside of the box of traditional business practices.

She currently resides in Denver, Colorado where she enjoys exploring the serenity of the Rocky Mountains.

For more information on Aligned For Action, LLC, or to contact the author, visit the website at:

www.alignedforaction.com
email: info@alignedforaction.com

Printed in the USA
CPSIA information can be obtained
at www.ICGtesting.com
LVHW091051090124
768520LV00004B/99